TIPPERARY TO TEXAS

TIPPERARY TO TEXAS

An Irish Family
Reunites After Four Generations

A MEMOIR

John F. Welsh Jr

iUniverse, Inc.
New York Lincoln Shanghai

TIPPERARY TO TEXAS
An Irish Family Reunites After Four Generations

iUniverse books may be ordered through booksellers or by contacting:

iUniverse
2021 Pine Lake Road, Suite 100
Lincoln, NE 68512
www.iuniverse.com
1-800-Authors (1-800-288-4677)

Because of the dynamic nature of the Internet, any Web addresses or links contained in this book may have changed since publication and may no longer be valid.

The views expressed in this work are solely those of the author and do not necessarily reflect the views of the publisher, and the publisher hereby disclaims any responsibility for them.

The poem *Life in Ireland* is reproduced with the permission of Mary Louise Welsh.

ISBN: 978-0-595-45356-6 (pbk)
ISBN: 978-0-595-69965-0 (cloth)
ISBN: 978-0-595-89669-1 (ebk)

Printed in the United States of America

For
My wife Mary

who brightens every room she enters.

Contents

Preface

BACK WHEN I was a young man, I was an ambitious newspaper reporter. It was a super job—something different happened every day, and there was never a boring minute. As a general assignment reporter, I seldom knew from day to day what story I would write. It could be interviewing a famous individual or some guy from down the street who could provide a human interest story; it could be covering some big convention in town; or it could be recording what was happening in the courthouse or at the police station, filling in for one of the "beat" reporters. Some of these assignments lasted only one day; others might drag out a little longer. It was whatever my city editor assigned me. The hours and days flew by.

That was fifty-plus years ago.

The *El Paso Herald-Post* was owned by the Scripps-Howard chain, and was one of the company's training grounds for beginning reporters. Not all the staff was in training—some of us were El Paso natives who had an education in journalism—but we had some turnover of new beginners, or of staff members who transferred or quit.

Some of our trainees were sons of East Coast newspaper executives. We had one whose dad was a celebrated editorial cartoonist for the *New York World-Telegram* and other Scripps-Howard papers, another whose dad was the Washington bureau chief for Scripps-Howard, and another whose dad was an editor of the *Washington Star*. But there was no problem with nepotism. We were all eager young newspaper reporters cranking out our assigned copy for an afternoon paper with a modest circulation in our mid-size border city. It was a great job.

Yes, it was a long time ago, but I remember most of it very well. You don't forget things about your first full-time job, especially when you loved every minute of it. You remember almost all of the people you worked with. You recall their idiosyncrasies—their good points as well as their annoying habits. You remember where their desks were located in the city room, and how you could usually spot their stories when they were printed in the paper because you recognized their style, even after our city editor finished his copyreading, sometimes marking up the story with his big, black copy pencil.

Our city editor was H. A. Michael. He will always be my most unforgettable character. Mike was a newspaperman from the so-called old school. He could be gruff; he could be gentle—especially to the female members of the staff. He could smile; he could frown. He could praise you one minute and then cuss you out the next. Every day he wore a clean, freshly pressed, starched shirt and a crumpled, stained necktie that he often used like a dishcloth or a face towel. He rolled his sleeve cuffs up two or three turns, and his belt was always about four inches too long. He carried his black lunch pail every day when he rode the downtown bus to work at 6:00 a.m. He constantly drank black coffee from his thermos, and his necktie carried coffee stains. He smoked Chesterfield cigarettes, the ends wet from being carried—often unlit—in his teeth most of the time. He could talk with his cigarette clamped between his front teeth. Most of us smoked, and we would imitate Mike with his lip-drenched Chesterfield. His ashtray on the semi-circular copy desk was always full of snuffed-out butts. It smelled awful, and it seldom, if ever, had been washed.

Being a charter member of the old school, Mike was not a connoisseur of literary prose. He was used to dealing in facts— bare facts—as he edited our stories. You could use a few adjectives here and there, or you might slip in an occasional compound or complex sentence, and you might attempt a little rhythm in your story, but it had better be basic. You know: who, what, where, when, why, and, perhaps, how—all in the lead paragraph. And he wanted it concise. Mike would have written *War and Peace* as a short story. He could have edited the King James Version of the Bible to fit on a postcard. In today's world, he would have compacted *60 Minutes* into 60 seconds.

It didn't take long for any of us to learn about how many words of copy our story should be. If our copy was too long, Mike used his big, black copy pencil, and we would have a hard time recognizing our story in print. Seldom, if ever, was any copy too short. We all learned a lot from Mike. For those who went on from the *Herald-Post* to bigger papers, the lessons learned from Mike were everlasting. He was the perfect guy to be boss over the reporters on a paper that trained apprentices. He was a teacher, a mentor, a coach—all wrapped into one. I loved the guy.

YOU HAVE PROBABLY heard or read somewhere that all newspaper people want to write a book. The Great American Novel. That is mostly true. After the final edition of the *Herald-Post* had gone to press every weekday afternoon, most of us retreated to the basement bar in the Hotel Cortez and had a few beers. We traded stories of the day's events, some of us mocked Mike, and we cussed and discussed some of the stories in our competing newspaper, the *El Paso Times*. We talked sports, bad-mouthed those uppity female staffers who seldom drank a beer with us, and, sometimes, talked about our hopes for the future—although that usually came after several beers. But, sooner or later, somebody would bring up writing his novel-of-the-future. His "book."

I wondered if those upcoming books were the result of Mike's dedication to brevity. After all, as the author, you probably would have some authority over the editor when you're writing your own book—you could expound when you wanted to; you could add adjectives and adverbs galore; compose a paragraph with five complex or compound sentences, if you wanted. You might even express your opinion. Your book editor might make a suggestion or do some editing of his own, but he had better use a small, black copy pencil with an eraser.

Of course, since all newspaper reporters believe they can write a book, they seriously doubt whether Nathaniel Hawthorne or John Dos Passos could cover a city council meeting as a reporter for the *Herald-Post*. Mike would eat Hawthorne's lunch; Passo's name would be Uno, not Dos.

On the other hand, all my compadres at the *Herald-Post* loved Ernie Pyle's many books. Maybe it was because each was a compilation of human interest stories that Ernie wrote as he traveled the country and endured the battlefields of Africa,

Europe, and the South Pacific. Ernie Pyle did not expound and did not write classic prose. He told his story in simple terms using simple words. Probably the fact that our city editor Mike and Ernie Pyle were friends and both veteran employees of the Scripps-Howard company had something to do with this since they probably received their early training from the same editor or a company manual.

At our late afternoon beer sessions, when the conversation got around to writing that book, I never said a word. Unlike the others, I never expressed the desire to write a book. To begin with, I didn't have the imagination to create some twisty plot involving fictitious characters located in some unfamiliar setting. It seemed to me that, after learning and following Mike's boil-it-down philosophy in the newsroom, it would be blasphemy to write a three hundred-page tale that rambled on and would take days for anyone to read.

*   *   *   *

BECAUSE OF THE historic low pay earned by newspaper people, I left the reporting field after a few years. And in the intervening fifty-plus years, I have never thought about writing a book, even though I have missed the writing. My literary activities have been confined to spur-of-the-moment letters to the editor or personal letters to family members living in distant places.

But my wife, Mary, has nagged me on more than one occasion to write a book about some of the interesting episodes in the history of my family—all the way back to a beginning in the mid-1800s in Ireland up through the intervening years. She has prevailed, and what follows is a compilation of various events in both Ireland and America—some related and some not—that occurred within my extended family. These events tell about the reuniting of my family after it was separated for over one hundred years because of emigration.

I hope that what follows would make Mike happy.

Introduction

THIS BOOK IS about two families—one American and one Irish—and how both have reunited since my wife, Mary, and I decided several years ago to trace my roots. This was not a big-time genealogical search in which we hired a firm in Ireland; it is one we did ourselves, and it is based upon information we have taken from old letters, church records, and the new County Heritage Centers in Ireland.

Additionally, this book pertains only to my father's family because his are the only relatives of mine that I know of who have kept track of one another over an extended period.

Prior to our recent coming-together in 1989, the two families had been separated for four generations—over one hundred years—because of emigration.

*   *   *   *

BEYOND THE PERIOD covered in this book, Ireland has both a wonderful and tragic history. It suffered during eight hundred years of rule by the English and, in many ways, still does. Deep down, most Irish still resent what happened during those eight hundred years. One of the things they will never forget is that millions of Irish citizens were forced to emigrate to America and to Australia. Many left because of the infamous and tragic potato famine. Many were found guilty of petty crimes, were marched onto ships, and were exiled to Australia. Still others left in search of better opportunity. And many emigrated to get away from religious persecution and severe bigotry.

The population of Ireland was eight million in the 1840s, but it dropped down to slightly over three million in the 1980s. However, in the late-1990s and early-2000s, the Irish economy improved greatly and many who left for America have returned. Today, Ireland is home to more than four million and its population continues to grow.

*   *   *   *

NOW ABOUT THE two families:

First, I'll deal with the American family. Counting me, this book will go back for four generations although I never knew my paternal grandfather or great-grandparents, and I certainly did not know their parents. But our research into the Welsh family includes them because they were the link that brought us together with our relatives in Ireland. And, as you will read, there are some members of the Welsh family who we know very little about. They seem to have dropped out of the picture, at least as far as the records that we have are concerned. I would like to know more about them and their offspring, and, if they have any interest in our family history, I would like to share information with them.

Second, this book basically deals with three generations of the Irish family, although the previous generation is included in some of the events we have recorded. The Irish family referred to in this book consists primarily of three of the eight children of Thomas Francis Jones and Mary Casey Jones: Mary Ann, Patrick, and Joanna. The father, Thomas, was an Englishman from Leeds who, it is claimed, had a royal appointment as vicar general of Jamaica, although, it is also claimed, he never visited the island—but it is a good tale.

Mary Ann, the firstborn, married John Francis Walsh, my great-grandfather, and together they had eight surviving children. They began emigrating from Ireland in 1888.

Patrick—forever known as Patsy—was Mary Ann's brother. He was also the father of fourteen children. His last child, Agnes Jones, married George Powell and was the mother of my five Powell cousins, the mainstays of the Irish family who have reunited with the American family.

Joanna, Mary Ann's younger sister, was the first Jones to leave for America, emigrating in about 1883. She married John King after she moved to St. Louis, and together they raised my grandfather, Michael Francis Welsh, and his seven siblings after their mother, Mary Ann, died in childbirth delivering stillborn twins. While raising Mary Ann's eight children, Joanna was also mother to five children of her own. In all, Joanna and John King raised thirteen children.

*   *   *   *

ALL OF THE events, stories, and sagas detailed are drawn from quite extensive research that Mary and I did during a fifteen-year period from 1989 to 2004. Virtually all of the tales are factual, either taken from personal records or having been verified with other relatives. There may be a few tales that are *probably* true, which are based again on conversations with members of one of the families. And, as we all know, the Irish are great storytellers.

The title *Tipperary to Texas* reflects the move of the Irish family from Ireland to settle in the American Southwest. Two of the core members of the original Jones family in Ireland did emigrate to the United States. One settled in Missouri and others eventually settled in Texas, including my grandparents. However, other offspring of the Jones family have stayed in Ireland and, except for a handful who have died recently, still reside in and around County Tipperary. The children of the Irish family are scattered around the island, but they remain closely knit. None are more than a few hours' drive from their parents or siblings. The children of the American family are scattered around the States, making reunions and visits more difficult because of greater distances between them.

Mary and I fell in love with Ireland after a few days during our first trip there in 1988. At that time and even today, in many ways, Ireland reminds me of America in the 1930s and early- 1940s before World War II when I was a young boy.

The Irish lifestyle is very different from the American lifestyle. The hustle-and-bustle, hectic pace in today's America has not reached Ireland, and I hope it never will. The Irish are more relaxed, more laid back, less concerned about world events, and less consumed by chasing the almighty dollar or euro. As one unknown Irish writer accurately put it, "The Irish do not live to work as some nations seem to do. The Irish only work to live and time is made for the good things in life: family, friends, the pub, recreation and sports."

THE TRANSATLANTIC TRAVEL route that stretches thousands of miles between the wild rhododendrons and the verdant green pastures of County Tipperary in Ireland to the mesquite bushes and dusty sand dunes of arid West Texas actually took shape for Mary and me on one of the pages in my dad's Bible.

Today, that Bible stands upright among other keepsake books on a shelf near the bottom of my bookcase. On several of the blank pages in the front of his Bible, Dad inscribed several notes like the ones you might find written for the ages in a formal family Bible.

I have read those notes occasionally since I was a teenager, but I never thought much about them. Almost twenty years ago when I stumbled across that Bible again, it dawned on me that I needed to explore those notes because Dad must have thought they were significant or he wouldn't have written them on those blank pages.

It would be a huge exaggeration to call that Bible a family Bible. It is not life-size like the one on a church's pulpit, it is a handier size, similar to those Gideon Bibles you find in the drawer under the telephone in every hotel and motel in America.

On the final blank page up front, in her best, unmistakable handwriting, my grandmother on my mother's side has written "To Johnnie Welsh Sr. from Mother and Hibbie. Christmas 1944." This gift is recorded for eternity.

*   *   *   *

IT WOULD BE safe to say that this was Dad's first Bible version of any kind. I had always assumed it was a King James Version. However, it doesn't say so anywhere that I could find.

Another Bible I have contains a detailed explanation that it is a product of James, King of Great Britain and other places, so I guess that one is a King James Version. Dad's Bible makes no such declaration, except that it is an authorized version. (I wondered if it was possible King James had an *un*authorized version?)

Yet another Bible I have says it is the New American Bible for Catholics. I found out after I had transitioned from Baptist to nothing to Roman Catholic about twenty years ago that the Catholic Bible is different from the King James Version, and that it is different for a lot of reasons including the extra books it contains—such as the Book of Tobit, the Book of Judith, the two Books of Macabees, Song of Songs (instead of Solomon), the Book of Wisdom, the Book of Sirach, and, lastly, the Book of Baruch.

It is almost as if King James Version is the Reader's Digest condensed edition because he cut out a lot of the books contained in the Catholic Bible. Maybe he didn't like the message they contained, but it does make it seem worthwhile to read those omitted books just to find out why King James gave them the heave-ho. (Perhaps that's where they list the Sins of Omission.)

*   *   *   *

DAD'S FAMILY WAS Irish Catholic. They attended Mass when it was very important, like Ash Wednesday, Good Friday, Easter, Christmas Eve Vigil, and maybe Christmas Day. The other Days of Obligation were passed over. So, with that not-too-strict religious background and upbringing, Dad was pretty much unchurched, as they say.

And on top of that, as a young man, he was dating and madly in love with Ernestyne Barganier, a El Paso High School sophomore from a hard-shell Southern Baptist family. It always seemed clear to me growing up that her matriarchal mother was third in command in the pecking order of the Baptist church, right after Jesus and John the Baptist, of course. She was devout.

When Dad's and Ernestyne's dating progressed from serious to let's-get-married, and after their attempt at elopement in nearby New Mexico was thwarted by the sheriff whom my grandmother had dispatched after them, she begrudgingly consented to their marriage—not to take place in the Baptist church because he was raised Catholic, but to be held in the bride's home—and only after Dad agreed that any children who should come along would be raised Southern Baptist. Being unchurched anyway, my dad, John, agreed to this condition and, besides that, it was better than being yanked from the Justice of the Peace's office by Sheriff Orndorf. When the ceremony took place, my dad had just turned nineteen years of age and my mom was barely sixteen.

So this brings us to the 1944 Christmas present my grandmother gave to my dad. I have no idea what went on between them religion-wise during that period from the marriage in 1926 to the gift in 1944, except that I know that I attended the First Baptist Church around the clock every single Sunday for twenty years.

✳   ✳   ✳   ✳

DAD USED THOSE blank up front pages of his Bible to make entries of important events: three lines each devoted to the highlights of my birth, my brother's birth, my marriage and the births of my children, my brother's marriage and the births of his children. There are some other entries about homes my dad and mom built and owned; dates that he and his brothers opened grocery stores, closed grocery stores, and sold grocery stores; a few facts about his mom and dad, my mom's dad and, finally, several entries about his family in Ireland.

The first entry about the Irish family notes that his grandfather's name was John Francis Welsh, and his grandmother's name was Mary Ann Jones. He wrote: "I have a cousin in Clonmel, Ireland, County Tipperary named Agnes Jones Powell. Michael F. Welsh (Dad's father) came from the County Cork harbor town of Dungarvan, which is directly south of Clonmel in Waterford County. We have relatives buried in the old cemetery by the old bridge in Clonmel. Mary Ann (the first child) is buried there."

Dad was recording information that his American cousin, Marcelline Welsh Braget, had passed along to him, but our research has shown that most of his entries are incorrect. It was John Francis W*a*lsh who was from Dungarvan in County Waterford; the cemetery is in the area of Clonmel called Old Bridge; the major portion of Clonmel is in County Tipperary; and it is Margaret Mary, not Mary Ann, who is buried there; Margaret Mary was the second born of John Walsh, not first.

*   *   *   *

THESE FINAL ENTRIES in Dad's Bible led Mary and me on a quest to dig out the roots of my family over the past almost twenty years. The results of this search have been very rewarding to us. The many relatives in Ireland that we have come to know have made our life better. I hope we have added something to theirs.

Let's begin.

CHAPTER ONE

Digging up
the Roots

IF YOU ARE looking up your roots, you need a family member like my cousin, Marcelline. She was the daughter of my grandfather's brother, and she lived with her husband, Walt Braget, and their two sons on a dairy farm on Puget Sound in Washington. I suppose she did all the things the wife of a dairy farmer does, but she did one thing that no one else in our family had ever done: she kept track of the Welsh family roots by exchanging letters with two relatives in Ireland, and her cousin Mary Margaret King in Missouri. And in 1982, when Marcelline became physically unable to continue the overseas pipeline, she passed her version of the family tree on to my wife, hoping Mary would realize that it had become her duty to carry on the connection between the Irish and American branches of the tree.

This family tree that Marcelline gave Mary was not like the ones you buy at the computer store. Instead, it was written in long, rambling letters of many pages. When she ran short of space, Marcelline wrote up and down the margins of the stationery and around the corners—everywhere. This bugged Mary, who is neat, orderly, well organized and who would never, ever write in the margins. So, one day while I was at work, she took all of Marcelline's many letters and transferred the family tree information onto huge sheets of art paper, which she had spread out across the living room floor. Mary was trying to make sense out of the correspondence between relatives living in Puget Sound and in County Tipperary.

Marcelline Welsh Braget (front) with John and Mary Welsh.

   Those few lines in my dad's Bible about having a cousin in Clonmel, County Tipperary, Ireland, had always been a mystery to me, even though my dad and I had never discussed it at all. So when Mary assembled all of Marcelline's information, it began to make some sense—at least to the point that I felt the responsibility to formalize the family tree so it could be passed along to our children, my brother and his children, and anybody else who was interested, including those family members whom I had never met who were still residing in Ireland. Yes, it was my duty to do this since I was the second oldest surviving American member of the Welsh family—sort of a self-proclaimed patriarch-in-waiting.

*   *   *   *

THE BEST WAY to nail down the family tree, it seemed to me, would be for Mary and me to take a short vacation to Ireland and combine sightseeing with research while introducing ourselves to the Irish kinfolk. So, in November 1987, Mary wrote a letter to Betty Powell Kelly in Clonmel, County Tipperary, telling her who we were and that we wanted to meet her and any other of the relatives who had been mentioned in Marcelline's letters when we would be in Ireland the following May.

Betty was the last member of the Irish family with whom Marcelline had corresponded. Before Betty and Marcelline took up the exchange of mail, the letters had been between their cousin, Mary Margaret King—who later became a nun in St. Louis and changed her name to Sister St. John—and Betty's mother, Agnes Jones Powell, who was my grandfather's cousin—the same Agnes Jones Powell referred to in my dad's Bible.

ABOUT THREE MONTHS after Mary sent her letter, we heard back from Betty. Her note was brief, written in classic Irish longhand, acknowledging Mary's letter, and adding that they would all be happy to meet us, especially after the many letters Betty had exchanged with Marcelline over the years. "Just let us know your travel plans," Betty wrote.

My five Irish cousins (left to right): Una Hayes, Betty Kelly, P. J. Powell, Joan Howlett, and Mary Frances Hazard.

Our travel plans called for two weeks in Ireland, and we had carefully scheduled each day. When we boarded the plane in West Texas, we knew what we were going to do each day: which sights we were going to see, which bed and breakfasts we were going to stay in, which three famous Irish golf courses we were going to play. We had our rental car lined up and a daily itinerary that allowed plenty of time for travel, sightseeing, and golf and adequate time to drink in all the Irish flavor and hospitality found in its renowned pubs—like the one we remembered from the movie *The Quiet Man*. We had scheduled more than three days in Clonmel for time with the kinfolk. Our reservations had been made at Clonmel's best hotel, according to Frommer's *Ireland on $30 a Day* travel book.

*   *   *   *

AFTER OUR LONG overnight flight from Atlanta to Shannon, we spent the remainder of that day and that night at a bed and breakfast in Ennis. The following morning, we began our Irish holiday.

As we twisted our way along the narrow Irish highways, dodging tiny cars, huge sheep, and monstrous trucks (they call them lorries), I wondered why anybody would leave such a beautiful place with such friendly people and move clear across the Atlantic to places like West Texas or Puget Sound. How could they leave the lifestyle? Oh, I had read a little about the Irish potato famine and the brutal English landlords and the breaking up of families and the coffin ships to America and Australia—but leave this place? It was love at first sight for both Mary and me. Yes, Ireland was all it was cracked up to be; it had good food (especially the brown bread and the desserts), friendly people (especially the ladies who operated their homes as bed and breakfasts), tasty drink (especially the Guinness and Murphy's stout), and great golf courses (especially Lahinch and Ballybunion).

For our sixth night, we had reservations at Ballygarry House, a small hotel on the outskirts of Tralee in County Kerry. We checked into our room during mid-afternoon, spent a couple of hours in the hotel's pub, and then drove back into Tralee to pick up snacks and a newspaper.

If you've driven in Ireland, or England for that matter, you know how confusing—and stressful—it can be to drive on the left side of the road, steering from the right side of the car and shifting gears with your left hand. I turned on the wipers while trying to use the turn blinkers; I turned on the lights without meaning to; I honked the horn when it wasn't necessary; and I freaked out the first time I entered a roundabout (a traffic circle).

So, it was not surprising when I made a wrong turn on the divided highway as we drove into Tralee for our snacks. The only way out of this blunder was to turn off the busy street onto a side road, drive into a housing area, and turn around—after catching my breath.

We had driven into a housing area containing what the Irish call "County Council" homes. It was what Americans call public housing—identical, two-story stucco buildings containing several apartments each. The buildings were all painted a dull gray color, built too close to each other, row after row, street after street. Even though it was still afternoon, men in their undershirts—obviously on the *dole* (welfare)—sat on the steps of the front entrances into the apartments; half-dressed kids played in the streets; dogs were everywhere; litter lined the curbs; and some clunker cars were jacked up on concrete blocks. What lawns there were had gone to seed, obviously untended. Weeds had sprouted up. There were a few window boxes, but few flowers. It was depressing; I couldn't turn around and drive out soon enough.

The neighborhood resembled a setting that I had seen before. I think it was on the evening news in a story about Catholics and Protestants who were killing one another in Belfast or

Derry in Northern Ireland. It was the same type of ghetto—and it was grim.

My mind began to spin. *My God,* I thought, *I know nothing about Betty Powell Kelly or the other relatives. Marcelline had never visited them, she had only written letters. We had not seen pictures of their homes or their neighborhoods or their automobiles. What kind of people are they? Not that we're so classy ourselves, but we don't sit on the front porch in undershirts, and our cars have four tires, all inflated. I mow the lawn weekly. We have flowers. What kind of folks are our relatives? Surely, they're not bomb-throwers or ghetto-dwellers, are they? Whoa! What lies ahead?*

*   *   *   *

FOR THE NEXT two days, I worried about meeting the family. We parked the car at our bed and breakfast in Killarney and took a bus tour around the Ring of Kerry, one of Ireland's top attractions. And, even though the scenery was gorgeous, I kept seeing the weeds and litter and banged-up cars along the highway instead of the many shades of green and the various shrubs and trees that seemed to be everywhere. I enjoyed the tour, but I was still apprehensive about my family.

The following day, we arrived in Clonmel after noon and checked into the Hotel Minella. Instead of calling Betty Powell Kelly immediately to tell her that we had arrived, we headed to the hotel's pub. I guess it was my delay game. I was procrastinating, and Mary shared my apprehension.

There were two gentlemen at the bar—an American and an Irishman—who had been at the Clonmel greyhound racetrack earlier that afternoon. We spent a lot of time talking with them, buying each other drinks, passing the time—stalling. But then, the hotel receptionist entered the pub to advise me that I had a telephone call, which she had put through into the bar. It was Betty.

"John," she said, "I hear ye just arrived and I hope your accommodations are satisfactory. We are expecting ye for tea (which I later found out meant supper) and my brother P. J. will pick ye up about half six (6:30 p.m.). Will that be okay, John?"

"Yes, Betty, that will be great," I answered. "We'll be ready."

She sounded okay: polite, but direct; friendly, but in charge. We finished our drinks, excused ourselves from our bar friends, and headed for our room to dress for tea at Betty's.

*   *   *   *

THE NEW OUTFIT that Mary had ordered from the Spiegel's catalogue looked great and so did she. She was putting her best foot forward for our Irish kinfolk. My blue blazer and striped necktie put me in good stead, so we walked down to the hotel's reception area and awaited P. J.'s arrival.

Soon enough, a slightly overweight, gray-headed man with a cane emerged from a Toyota four-door sedan, and came up the steps, one at a time. He reminded me of Edward Arnold or Gene Lockhart—the old-time movie actors who always played the parts of mayor or governor or shady CEOs. He was wearing gold-rimmed glasses and a loose-fitting fisherman's sweater. He had thick jowls, a rosy complexion, and a big smile on his face. I guessed him to be in his sixties.

"John," he said. "Mary. I'm your cousin P. J. Let's head to the bar."

No problem, I thought. *He seems like an affable guy: dressed okay, outgoing, seems happy to see us. The bar's okay with me.* Mary was two steps ahead, walking beside P. J. We were the only ones in the bar—our greyhound fans had left.

Author John Welsh and his Irish cousin, P. J. Powell
get acquainted at the Hotel Minella bar.

We went through the conversation you would expect. "Tell me about your trip so far ... Are you used to the traffic yet and the left side of the road? Is your rental car okay? How did you find the B and Bs? Have you enjoyed the Guinness? What did you think of the Ring of Kerry? Isn't it gorgeous? How long will you be with us?"

P. J. was sizing us up; we were sizing him up. *So far, so good.*

*   *   *   *

AS WE STARTED our second round of drinks, the hotel receptionist entered the bar.

"Mister Powell," she said. "I have a phone call for you in the lobby."

P. J. didn't move.

"That would be Betty," he replied. "Tell her we're on our way."

The receptionist headed back to her desk, but she returned immediately.

"Mister Welsh," she said. "Missus Kelly wants to talk to you."

I went to the phone.

"Now John, I know P. J. like a book," she exclaimed. "I'm putting this straight up to ye. Our tea is ready, and I'm expecting ye to leave the hotel straight away," she said. "We'll be expecting ye shortly, John."

When I returned to our table in the pub, I explained to P. J. that Betty seemed upset and that I thought it would be good if he would drive us on to her home. He agreed—rather reluctantly—and we finished our drinks and drove to the Kelly home in P. J.'s Toyota.

*   *   *   *

CLONMEL IS A beautiful town of about eighteen thousand people. It straddles the River Suir, which puts the northern part of town in County Tipperary and the southern part in County Waterford. The town is situated between the Galtee and the Knockmealdown mountains, and, nearby, a large mountain named Slievenamon looms above the pastured fields. All of the valleys around Clonmel are dairy farm country—some of Ireland's best cheese is produced there. It is famous for its salmon fishing and for its crystal clear small streams and creeks, like the

River Suir as it surges downstream toward the Celtic Sea at Waterford. The swift-flowing river, the rock-bordered pastures below the scenic mountains, and the town of Clonmel are truly postcards come alive.

We crossed the Suir, skirted the downtown area, and drove about two miles to the Kelly bungalow on the northwest side of town. The house was only a few years old and its exterior was brick and plaster construction. A matching brick and plaster wall ran around the entire property. The lawn and garden were partially completed. A curb outlined where the driveway would be and shrubs and several colorful trees were thriving. The area to be grassed was being prepared for planting: the soil had been turned under and carefully raked. Some fertilizer had been spread in preparation for sod. The driveway was covered in small gravel.

Two large complexes of buildings were located across the street on a large, park-like piece of property. The land behind and on each side of the house was undeveloped, but it had been neatly mowed earlier and was covered with wild flowers.

Betty met us at the door. You could immediately see the family resemblance to P. J. She was in her sixties and neatly dressed. Her one-time reddish hair was streaked with gray, and she had that same rosy Irish complexion as P. J. She also had the same big smile. There were no handshakes—she hugged us both and then scolded P. J. for delaying our tea. Betty's husband, Mick, was in the kitchen, finishing up the food preparation. Mick was not a large man like P. J., but he was very fit. He seemed shy, but friendly. He seemed to give way to P. J. and Betty. He had on his Sunday best—a striped dress shirt and necktie, pressed trousers, and freshly shined shoes. He had a firm handshake and immediately made eye contact—I knew right then that Mick and I would become good friends over time.

Mary Welsh (left) with Betty Kelly in front of Old Bridge House in Clonmel.

Betty was worried that her food would be spoiled, so she did her best to usher P. J. out the door. And, as he left, he remarked: "John. Mary. Enjoy your tea. We will all gather later tonight at Eldon's and the real drinking will begin." After an afternoon in one bar with a substantial number of drinks already under our belts, those were words we had not expected. But, you know, when in Rome ...

*   *   *   *

BETTY'S TEA TURNED out to be a treat of a cold supper— fresh salad with very tasty tomatoes and leaf lettuce, fresh salmon caught that day from the River Suir only a few blocks away, potato salad, and freshly warmed brown bread with real butter from the local creamery. We had hot tea and an apple tart for dessert. It was wonderful. Betty seemed relieved that her guests had enjoyed the supper.

Afterwards, we cleared the table and gathered in a den area that was part of the kitchen. Our small talk was unrestrained, and it was as if we had known one another for years. Mick's shyness was gone and his sense of humor exposed itself. He poured us all a small after-dinner drink of Irish Mist and recited an appropriate toast, ending with a sly, sheepish grin.

Mick had only recently retired from a position as the farming superintendent for the two government-operated hospitals across the street. Much of the hospitals' food needs were raised on the farming areas behind the hospitals; its milk and meat were, so to speak, homegrown. Mick had been the superintendent for many years, and he was provided a home owned by the hospitals as a part of his benefits. As Mick's retirement neared, he had purchased land from the hospital board and he and Betty had built their own retirement home.

Although he was now in his seventies, Mick himself had done all the landscaping and the preparation for the lawn. He had positioned the curbing bricks before having the gravel base hauled in for the driveway. The asphalt would be laid in June when the weather was more predictable.

Mary and Betty hit it off immediately that night. Betty was a little older than me and about ten years older than Mary. She was the second daughter of George and Agnes Jones Powell. Joan Howlett was the eldest, then Betty, then Una Hayes, then Peter Joseph (P. J.), and finally Mary Frances Hazard. As the only son, P. J. had years before proclaimed himself patriarch of the family, and everyone seemed to recognize his position, unless, of course, they didn't want to. That was the family arrangement, and it was okay with everyone, even the husbands of Joan, Betty, and Una. Mary Frances was divorced—which had created a family crisis many years before—then remarried, and was later widowed. At the time Mary and I met with Betty, Mick, and P. J., Mary Frances was a nurse living in London who visited her siblings as often as possible.

After we had visited for a while, Mary handed Betty and Mick small gifts that we had brought from Texas. We gave Betty a Texas wind chime that had bluebonnets, the state flower, handpainted on the chimes. We presented Mick with a jar of Mexican jalapeño jelly that tasted both hot and sweet—a taste unique in Ireland at that time.

At 9:30 (half nine in Ireland), we adjourned to Eldon's bar where, as P. J. had stated, the real drinking was scheduled to begin.

Time Capsule
1860 to 1890

America: The Civil War erupts after the Southern states secede from the Union. Millions of Americans are killed and wounded during the course of the war. Secretary of State Seward arranges the purchase of Alaska from Russia for $7,200,000. Outlaws Frank and Jesse James plunder the West. The Fifteenth Amendment gives African Americans the right to vote. President Andrew Johnson issues blank amnesty, pardoning all who participated in the Confederacy.

Ireland: The worst years of the potato famine pass. Charles Parnell of Mayo, elected as Member of Parliament, backs Irish tenant farmers seeking land reform, but he begins a torrid, infamous affair with Kitty O'Shea, falls out of favor with his constituents, loses three elections, and dies in 1891. British Prime Minister William Gladstone disestablishes the Protestant Church in Ireland. Unrest grows. A watered-down land reform bill is passed later.

Family: After losing his job as barrel-maker for Murphy's, John Walsh and part of his family join his wife, Mary Ann's sister, Joanna, and her husband in St. Louis. Mary Ann brings their other seven children to America, but dies later in childbirth. John abandons the eight surviving children to an orphanage, but Joanna moves them to her home in Hannibal, where the children join her, her husband, John King, and their five children. She begins to raise all thirteen to maturity.

CHAPTER TWO

The Social Center

ELDON'S WAS OUR family's Irish pub. They all went there as a matter of course and had been going there for years and years. Yes, they would visit other drinking establishments, but it was the "family's pub," which is a normal thing in Ireland. Every family has its favorite pub that the family frequents. As a result, they know just about everyone who goes there and it is as much a social center as a bar. True, children cannot be in a pub after about 7:30 p.m., but almost all Irish families take the children with them to their pub every Sunday after noon Mass where they can socialize with their friends until the pubs close at 2:00 p.m. for two hours, allowing time for the families to return home for Sunday dinner.

Pubs play a big part in Irish culture, and that is a good thing. The patrons share small talk, tell humorous stories, keep up with one another, and generally have a good time as they have a few drinks. I read an apt description somewhere "Irish pubs breathe a sense of warmth—and belonging—which is equaled in few countries."

The pub owner and barmen keep a close eye on all the patrons. They make sure no one has a near-empty glass, but they won't allow anyone to over-drink. You don't see many drunks in Irish pubs.

Eldon's is just such a pub. It is located near downtown Clonmel. Its owner Eldon Morris lives with his wife and family in quarters above the pub. He has an adjoining liquor store (called an "off-license" in Ireland) and a large, secure parking lot for his patrons. Like at *Cheers*, the television bar in Boston, everybody knows your name at Eldon's.

His patrons are primarily an older set, generally in their fifties and older. Most of them have been Eldon's customers for years, since back when they were in their twenties and thirties, and they have all grown older together. At that time of our first visit (the pub has since been remodeled), Eldon's was deco 1960s. It had booths of various sizes covered in gold-colored vinyl. All the woodwork was stained oak, and the cushions on the small portable stools were covered in a paisley pattern. The television was mounted up on the wall, but it was never turned on in the evenings when patrons were there. Only the afternoon pub patrons, the few that there were, watched TV. One exception to that rule would be a prime-time sporting event.

*   *   *   *

PRACTICALLY ALL OUR Clonmel relatives were there when we arrived at Eldon's with Betty and Mick. In his take-charge style, P. J. had commandeered the biggest booth, shoving in additional tables and stools.

Una and Seamus Hayes, P. J. and his wife, Esther, his daughter, Áine, and Áine's fiancé, Kevin O'Dwyer, were already there. They seemed to be anxious to meet their Yank cousins. After the introductions were out of the way, P. J.'s "real" drinking began.

As is the custom at most Irish pubs, the patrons place their own orders at the bar and serve themselves—there are no waitresses serving the tables and booths. Seamus explained that it was customary for the men to take turns buying rounds, and each placed and picked up the orders when his turn came up. I had the feeling that you weren't allowed to say "no" to another drink. When a new round was brought to the table, there was a drink for everyone whether the previous drink was finished or not.

All the men were drinking pints of Guinness, the ladies were sipping Paddy's, a popular Irish whiskey, chased down with water. The whiskey and water were not mixed at the bar; the water was served on the side in a small glass pitcher. The shot of Paddy's was served in a wine glass. Ice cubes were optional.

Although Mary is no pansy when it comes to drinking, I noticed her Paddy's were backing up, and she finally called time-out, bringing laughter from the rest. She eventually caught up, and the relatives learned the time-out signal you see at American basketball games.

All the jokes, stories, and tales you hear in Irish pubs are called *craic*, pronounced "crack." That was our first exposure to hours of *craic*, but, sitting there taking it all in, the *craic* was great, and it is one of the features of my Irish experience that I will never forget.

I kept up with my Irish kinfolk drinking Guinness that night, and I can assure you it is difficult to get very drunk from the stout. It is filling, and even though my four pints of Guinness equaled an entire half-gallon, I felt great. It was a super first night with our relatives, and I was no longer apprehensive.

As the conversations continued, we learned something about each of our relatives. Seamus Hayes was the county manager for the southern half of County Tipperary, called the "south riding." The position of county manager is somewhat of a bureaucratic-appointed civil service position rather than a political appointment. Seamus worked his way up through lesser assignments in smaller counties, eventually becoming the assistant county manager for County Wicklow, and, when the position became open, was named county manager for Tipperary South in Clonmel, both his and Una's hometown. The county manager controls local funds, supervises department heads, and carries out all decisions and regulations made by the elected county board.

Conversation at Eldon's Pub in Clonmel, County Tipperary. Esther Powell talks with John Welsh and P. J. Powell (right).

P. J. had served many terms as an elected alderman on Clonmel's Town Council. There the aldermen elect the mayor from their group, and P. J. had served two terms as mayor. A picture of him, in formal robes wearing the ornamental chains, hangs in the Clonmel Town Hall. For many years, he was one of the recognized leaders of the conservative Irish political party, *Fine Gael*. At election time, aspiring politicians all met privately with P. J., seeking both his advice and endorsement. He loved politics.

Mick had been the farm superintendent, but he was very quiet about his politics. In later years he confided to me that he favored *Fianna Fail*, the more liberal Irish political party. He proudly stated that he was a "de Valera man," a term dating back to the Irish Civil War in the early-1920s. When the award-winning movie about the future Irish president Eamonn de Valera's rival *Michael Collins* was screened in 1996, Mick refused to see the movie even though it was acclaimed as the best movie ever to depict Ireland's independence from England and its struggle between being a free state or a republic. Politics, especially for the old-timers, is serious business in Ireland to this day. Grudges stem from differences dating back eighty years; they are seldom forgotten or forgiven. Hard feelings are more pronounced in Northern Ireland between the majority Protestants and the minority Catholics, but a lesser feeling of enmity exists in Ireland between *Fine Gael* and *Fianna Fail* stalwarts, most of whom take politics in stride.

As an appointed county official whose job was secure regardless of which political party was in control at any given time, Seamus was non-committal on politics. He would much rather talk about golf or his six children.

Neither Betty nor Esther nor Una worked outside the home. Each of them had a large home and a large family—all of their children were grown. Each woman loved to cook, and they enjoyed the evenings at Eldon's with their husbands and the friends they would meet at the pub. They socialized with one another only on a from time-to-time basis such as our visit or a holiday, but they were proud of their family's place in Clonmel and its role in the town's history.

Only three of the Powell siblings were at Eldon's, the other two lived elsewhere. The eldest, Joan, lived in Galway with her husband, Sean Howlett, who was assistant county manager of County Galway. The youngest, Mary Frances, lived in a suburb of London and worked as a nurse. My wife and I met both sisters later, and they were just as outgoing and friendly as Betty, Una, and P. J.

After that first day, there was one thing of which Mary and I were certain—these Irish relatives did not sit on the front porch in their undershirts, all their tires were inflated, and there were no concrete blocks. Whew!

*   *   *   *

THE FOLLOWING DAY, P. J. picked us up at our hotel mid-morning for a tour of the back roads around Clonmel. We drove through the nearby green valleys, all of them abounding with dairy farms. We drove along the gorgeous River Suir, crossed some of its old stone bridges, and stopped at small pubs in villages in Counties Tipperary and Waterford. Having been a pub owner himself many years before, and having his hand in politics, P. J. knew every pub owner in the area—and they knew him. He made us feel like celebrities when he introduced us to his acquaintances.

Our visit to Clonmel lasted another two days, and we crowded as much into those days as we could. We continued to pick up tidbits about family history and were able to verify and add on to the family tree that Mary was maintaining. When we left Clonmel, we were overcome with the friendliness of these relatives and the open-armed acceptance they gave us. We were proud to be part of their family, and we seemed to have been welcomed into it.

We wound up our trip in Dublin after many stops along the way. Each day brought a new love for Ireland—we were completely taken back by the beauty of the country, how helpful the people are to tourists, and the genuine love the Irish people have for Americans. Their welcome to travelers is sincere.

By the time we headed home, our search for my roots was well underway, and we carried it one step further eighteen months later when we made our second trip to Ireland.

∗   ∗   ∗   ∗

DURING THE INTERIM between trips, I searched the Internet for more information and wrote letters to various Irish governmental agencies and publications concerning citizenship. I found that Irish law allowed children and grandchildren of its citizens to obtain Irish citizenship through a program called Foreign Births Registration. If a child or grandchild of a citizen was born outside of Ireland, the law considered that they were simply born outside their country, even though their residency could be in another nation. I fell within the law and, incidentally, found out there were some governmental benefits that I would be eligible to use should I obtain dual citizenship.

This research showed that I had to obtain certified copies of the birth certificates for my grandfather, my father, and me. Mine had to show a link to my father, and his had to show a link to his father, and my grandfather's had to have been issued by an Irish records agency.

In 1989, our second trip provided the opportunity for me to obtain my grandfather's birth certificate and learn more about his parents and brothers and sisters. During that trip, I wanted more than just comments from relatives about our history—I sought out verifiable genealogical records that would prove my links to the Irish family.

Mary and I scheduled only a token amount of sightseeing for the second trip, and we settled in at a bed and breakfast up the street from Betty and Mick's home in Clonmel. We spent time with the church clerk at the Sts. Peter and Paul Catholic Church there and were able to view the actual records of my great-grandparents' marriage in 1875 and the baptism of my grandfather in 1881—all having taken place in the same church building.

At that time, all marriage, baptismal, and death records that were kept in each Catholic parish throughout Ireland were being transferred from huge, dusty record books to computer-ized data banks by employees of newly-authorized Heritage Centers in each of Ireland's twenty-six counties. The records from Sts. Peter and Paul Church that pertained to parishioners living in the Waterford County section of Clonmel had been transferred to a heritage center in Waterford City, only twenty-two miles south.

Obtaining my grandfather's birth certificate at the County Waterford Clerk's Office was rather easily done. P. J himself wanted to obtain the records of the births and baptisms of my grandfather's brothers and sisters. P. J. made a couple of preliminary phone calls from Clonmel, and then we all spent a few hours in Waterford City. We ended up with a lengthy printout that verified parentage, marriage dates, and baptismal dates of all the children born to John Francis Walsh and Mary Ann Walsh (née Jones). The printout showed brothers and sisters that Marcelline hadn't known about or included in her letters. The names of godparents of each child were even listed on the baptismal records.

After Mary and I studied the birthdates of John and Mary Ann's children, we were able to verify the dates of emigration from Ireland that we had compiled from other sources. We were elated. And P. J. was elated—up to when he saw that printout, I am not sure he was fully convinced of our relationship to his family. To show how excited and happy he was, he arranged a Mayor's Reception in the chambers of the Clonmel Town Hall in our honor.

*   *   *   *

P. J. AND HIS wife, Esther, scheduled a Saturday morning trip to the town hall under the guise of showing us some of the plaques and pictures of the town of Clonmel from when he was alderman and, on two different occasions, mayor. We were told that I should wear a coat and tie, and Mary should wear an appropriate dress, much like town hall employees wore to work.

P. J. and Esther's son-in-law-to-be Kevin O'Dwyer knew that we had a video camera with us, and asked if we would like for him to record our tour of the town hall. We readily agreed, thinking that a video of the town hall with pictures of Mary and me and P. J. and Esther would be interesting to our children and friends back home.

The five of us arrived at about 10:00 a.m., and as soon as we entered the lobby of the town hall, we were surrounded by other relatives and several men decked out in medieval-type velvet robes. Not all of the bedecked men were strangers to us—we had met most of them in Eldon's pub on our first night in Clonmel some eighteen months previous, and others we had met at the Clonmel Golf Club earlier in the week.

P. J. Powell, Mary Welsh, Mayor Sean Nyhan, John Welsh
At Mayor's Reception in Clonmel Town Hall.

We were greeted by Mayor Sean Nyhan and his five aldermen: Ted Lyons, Billy Byrne, Tommy Norris, Ted Boyle, and

John Kennedy. Our cousin, Seamus Hayes, was there both as a relative and as the County Tipperary county manager.

We were seated at the head table with Mayor Nyhan and P. J. The aldermen and our relatives were seated at tables arranged in a rectangle facing the head table, and there were about twenty people in all. The mayor's chair was papal in size. Mary and I will never forget the comments that the town officials and P. J. made during the reception.

After proper introductions were made, the mayor officially welcomed us to Clonmel and assured us that our welcome was more than cursory. He reminded us that our cousin P. J. had been a leader in the community for many years, and was one of the most respected men in the Clonmel area—as were the members of the entire Powell and Jones extended families, he quickly added.

Then P. J. took the floor. He told everyone that we had all gone to Waterford earlier in the week to "search out John's roots" and obtain a listing of our ancestors from records at the Sts. Peter and Paul Church that had been transferred to the computers at the Waterford Heritage Center.

"We found irrevocable evidence that John and Mary are closely tied to the Jones and Powell families and, in fact, to the Clonmel community," he told everyone. "We have the proof," he continued, "that John's grandfather, Michael, was born in Old Bridge House (then the residence of P. J. and Esther) many years ago. As a young lad, Michael accompanied his mother and father, Mary Ann and John Walsh, to America where they moved in with his mother's sister, Joanna.

"And, what is most important, John plans to cement his ties to his Irish family. Next week, John and Mary will travel to Dublin to apply for his Irish citizenship."

P. J. is a longtime politician and knows how to make a speech. As he spoke his volume ranged from fairly loud and direct to almost whisper-like soft and slow. When he completed the part about our seeking Irish citizenship, Mary and I received a standing ovation. It was very moving. Then the *craic* began.

P. J. told everyone that Patsy, the town's cooper, had trained John's great-grandfather as his apprentice, teaching him how to make wooden barrels that could be used to contain Murphy's Stout, brewed in Clonmel at that time. Patsy was P. J.'s grandfather.

Some of the stories that followed provoked one laugh after another, and the reception culminated with a speech from Alderman John Kennedy who rambled on and on about Clonmel politics, Irish politics, and his devotion to the Clonmel Cemetery Restoration Committee. He tied his own family into the Jones and Powell families, and commented that he wasn't sure whether that was "*genealogy* or *gynecology*." When he finally wound up his will-he-ever-finish comments, Aldermen Tommy Norris sprung to his feet.

"It must have been gynecology," Alderman Norris exclaimed. "It took you so long to deliver!" Needless to say, that brought down the house.

Following Alderman Kennedy's speech, we remarked on how much we appreciated the reception. Referring back to the relationship between Patsy and my great-grandfather as coopers, I told the group that it was gratifying to find out that, after all these years, some of my ancestors had actually made the barrels that the succeeding generations of the Welsh family had spent so much time in emptying.

During the event, we were presented with a large, framed plaque commemorating, in Old English script, "our visit to the town of John's ancestors," appropriately signed by all members of the town council, as well as P. J. and Seamus.

Mayor Sean Nyhan, County Manager Seamus Hayes, Esther Powell, and Una Hayes at Mayor's Reception.

The formal portion of the reception, and the *craic* that followed, ended and the party began. A huge table of food and drink had been set up at the opposite end of the council's chambers. Irish whiskey, Guinness, and Harp Lager were in big supply, along with coffee and hot tea. Sandwiches and dessert tarts were stacked on trays, and informal conversations were underway throughout the room.

P. J. took us to one of the long walls in the room and showed us the plaques that listed mayors and aldermen stretching back for over three hundred years. He proudly showed us the ornamental chains worn by the mayors over the years. The original chain is made of gold and is only worn within the chambers when the council is in session, or during an official Mayor's Reception such as ours. A less expensive replica is worn outside the town hall when appropriate.

The Mayor's Reception was a wonderful gesture on P. J.'s part. And Kevin, who had asked us about the video camera, recorded the entire event.

Today, when we are a little homesick for Clonmel and our Irish family, we pull out Kevin's video and relive that morning. We still laugh at the gynecology remark, and I surely wish I had known Patsy Jones.

*   *   *   *

OUR SECOND TRIP to Ireland wound up a few days after the Mayor's Reception, but we still needed to go to the citizenship offices in Dublin.

With all three required birth certificates in hand, Mary and I traveled to the agency in Dublin that handled citizenship applications. When we inquired there, we were told that a change of procedure had taken place and that we would have to apply at the Irish consulate nearest to our home in West Texas, which turned out to be in Chicago. We left the agency disappointed, but at least we knew what our next step would be. We could take care of that when we returned home to Texas.

*   *   *   *

DURING THE MAYOR'S Reception, P. J. announced that his daughter Áine and Kevin, soon to be married, would be moving to California, where Kevin had been transferred by a software affiliate of Lockheed, the giant aircraft manufacturer. Within several months, Áine and Kevin were living in Orange County, soaking up the wonderful Southern California sun. Soon they had their first guests visit.

Áine's sister, Fiona, and her husband, Sean O'Keeffe, arrived, planning to stay for several weeks. Sean is an officer in the Irish Army and Fiona had been a fashion designer before she became a mother. Since Mary and I were in close contact with the California cousins, we urged all four of them to hop onto a plane and fly into El Paso, our nearest large airport. They jumped at the chance; they had all seen enough Western movies that made them anxious to visit Texas and the Mexican border.

Earlier that year, Mary and I had built a small Pueblo-style second home about ninety miles south of Alpine, Texas, in a new golf resort named Lajitas. It is located on the Rio Grande River on the western edge of the Big Bend National Park, and we retreated there for long weekends. Lajitas is in an area that always has one of the hottest daytime temperatures in the country, but, at the same time, it has extremely low humidity. It is hot and dry and a slight breeze makes it very pleasant year around. It seldom rains.

Our cousins' flight from California arrived at about midnight. We picked them up to drive them to our home in the mountains south of Alpine so we could all spend a few days there and in Lajitas. They had missed their evening meal because of a long drive to the airport and they said they were starved. We stopped at a very large Petro Truck Stop that contains an outstanding restaurant, The Iron Skillet, on the way out of El Paso. At that late hour, it was the ideal place to eat.

While the other three chose sandwiches, Fiona ordered a chicken fried steak. When I have ordered a chicken fried steak in a truck stop restaurant, it is always about the size of a pizza and usually has a mountain of mashed potatoes, a ladle of brown gravy, and a stack of green beans. It is a meal big enough for, well, a truck driver. Fiona's was no different.

Our orders arrived, and everyone "dug in." Somebody raved about the thick Texas toast used on the club sandwich, another loved the thick slices of ham and the American cheese slices, but Fiona appeared unsure about her chicken fried steak.

"How is it?" I asked.

"Oh, it tastes great," she replied. "It just doesn't taste like chicken!"

Mary and I broke into laughter. I explained that it wasn't chicken—it was a steak that was breaded the same way chicken was usually breaded. I assured her it was Texas beef that she was eating and that it was top quality.

My comments didn't matter. She loved it, and she probably consumed more of that truck stop chicken fried steak than any five foot two—maybe one hundred-pound—ex-Irish fashion designer had ever eaten.

After the meal, we drove the remaining three hours to our Alpine home. It was still springtime and a little cool for swimming, but our Irish visitors were used to cooler weather and they spent several hours of the next day in our pool and on the deck, sunning and enjoying margaritas and Bud Light beer.

Bright and early the following morning, we left for Lajitas. I had made arrangements for rental golf clubs for Kevin and Sean, and the three of us headed straight for the course. Mary and the girls went to the Lajitas pool. We repeated the same schedule the morning after that.

Our son, Joseph, joined us from Alpine to make a foursome. We iced down beer and loaded a cooler onto one of the golf carts. Since it was midday—and very hot with little breeze—the beer did not last long. When we passed by the golf shop at the end of nine holes, I phoned Mary at our house and asked her to bring us another cooler full of beer. Kevin was ecstatic.

"Perfect, John," he shouted from the cart. "What a life. You play golf, ride in a cart, have warm weather and no rain. And, best of all, when you run out of beer, you just pick up your mobile and dial 1-800-BUD LIGHT, and here comes Mary with a full cooler!"

After sunning and swimming at the Lajitas pool for several hours, Mary and the two girls returned to the house. The thermometer on our back porch showed 116 degrees—and that was in the shade. The Irish girls, back from the pool, saw the reading and couldn't believe their eyes.

"A hundred and sixteen! My God," Áine screamed.

"Yes, but it *is* dry," Mary answered. "Stay inside. I'm going to run this beer down to the guys. I'll be right back."

When she returned, Mary didn't see either Áine or Fiona in the living room, but she soon heard them. They had filled up the bathtub with cold water and both of them had crowded into it with the water up to their necks. They had found the solution to the Lajitas heat.

The next day the six of us—Joseph had returned to Alpine—headed back to El Paso, stopping several times along the scenic highway next to the Rio Grande between Lajitas and Presidio for photo opportunities, then crossing into Mexico for a quick peek at Ojinaga. We arrived at the airport in plenty of time for our kinfolk to make their flight back to Southern California.

I suppose their short trip was memorable: to Kevin and Sean because of the personal delivery service and the Bud Light on the golf course, and to Áine and Fiona for the 116 degrees and the cold icy bath. It is likely that Fiona also remembered the chicken fried steak. And, for Mary and I, our best memory was of the close fellowship we shared with them—we all got to know each other better.

*   *   *   *

IT HAD BEEN a time-consuming project to obtain two of the required three birth certificates of my grandfather, Michael Francis Walsh, my dad, John Francis Welsh, and myself. Mine, of course, was easy—I had umpteen copies that I had obtained on previous occasions.

Mary (top) with P. J. and Esther Powell's daughters: Orla, Áine, and Fiona.

Michael Walsh's birth certificate was easy to obtain as well. During our second trip to Ireland, we had traveled to the County Waterford clerk's office and given the attendant the information we had obtained from Sts. Peter and Paul Church and the Waterford Heritage Center. After reviewing several records and requiring a small fee, the attendant gave us a certified copy of my grandfather's birth records that showed his name as Michael Francis Walsh. He was born September 29, 1881, in the St. Mary's parish district in Old Bridge in County Waterford. His father was John Walsh. His mother was Mary Ann Walsh. His father's occupation was listed as cooper. His birth was officially registered on October 7, 1881, by Joanna Jones (Mary Ann's sister) who, it was noted on the birth certificate, signed with "X, her mark," certifying her presence at the birth. Michael's birth certificate gave us two of the three we needed.

I knew that my dad was born in Hannibal, Missouri, on September 11, 1907, to Michael and Nellie Gray Welsh. We wrote to the Marion County clerk, but found that the State of the Missouri only started keeping records in 1910 and that all local records before that year had been destroyed in a county courthouse fire. We felt like we had met a stone wall, but another letter from the courthouse that we received the following week revealed that, if we could provide affidavits verifying his birthplace and date, we could receive what the State of Missouri called "a delayed process" birth certificate.

My dad's brother Bob, who lived nearby in El Paso, and their first cousin Marcelline, signed the affidavit I sent them, making sure to have it notarized. I packaged the application for the birth certificate and the two affidavits together and mailed it to the secretary of state's office in Jefferson City, Missouri. Within a few weeks, a certified copy of the delayed process birth certificate arrived.

I had all I needed for Irish citizenship.

On September 26, 1990, my official application for foreign birth registry together with the three birth certificates and my check in the amount of $153 for processing was mailed to the consulate general of Ireland in Chicago. The processing took about six months, but on March 12, 1991 I received notification that my name had been duly entered into the Foreign Births Register. I now held dual Irish and American citizenship. Mary and I celebrated the occasion with a couple pints of Guinness.

In a little more than two years, we had dug up some of my roots. We had made two trips to Ireland, met scores of our cousins, and made dozens of new friends. I had even obtained Irish citizenship which was very important to me, as it still is today.

Exactly three years after I had received my Irish citizenship, Mary became eligible for postnuptial citizenship because I was an Irish citizen. She had to produce affidavits from various sources verifying that we had been married for more than three years and that we shared the same household. She had to furnish a copy of our marriage license and a copy of the certificate of registration of our marriage in Colorado. This process took about three months.

As I recall, we downed a few cans of Guinness Draft in celebration of that occasion too. We telephoned the relatives in Ireland to join us in absentia at Eldon's: I told them: "Order me a pint and Mary will have a Paddy's with water on the side. Skip the ice."

As I THOUGHT about the dual citizenship status and what it meant to the both of us, my mind kept drifting back to the events that had brought those first few members of the Jones family to emigrate from their homeland. They became the starting point for the Welsh family.

Events that led to the establishment of the Welsh family began in Clonmel with—what else?—pints of Irish stout.

Time Capsule
1890 to 1910

America: Congress passes the Sherman Anti-Trust Act to impose controls on monopolies, but ironically it prevents unions from taking collective action. After losing a one-sided war, Spain grants independence to Cuba, cedes Puerto Rico and Guam to the U.S., and the U.S. purchases the Philippines from Spain for $20,000,000. Work begins on the Panama Canal. Immigrants amount to 15 percent of the U.S. population, and they are "a despised class of people."

Ireland: The second attempt for a Home Rule Bill granting Ireland limited freedom passes in the British House of Commons, but it is vetoed in the House of Lords. Its debate widens the breech between Ulster and rest of Ireland. The new Gaelic League opposes "Anglicization," pushing for Irish athletics, Irish clothes, Irish dances, and Irish poetry and song to change the culture from *Englishness* to *Irishness*—a movement that becomes political.

Family: Michael Welsh, second son of John and Mary Ann Walsh, marries Nellie Gray and works as a railroad engineer in Hannibal, Missouri. His switch engine hauls ore and materials into a cement plant, but the dust and particles damage his lungs and start the breakdown of his health. His first son, John Francis Welsh, is born. Michael's father, who had abandoned the family in 1891, surfaces in Chicago, unable to hold a job and drinking heavily.

CHAPTER THREE

Two Free Pints

JUST LIKE ITS major competitor Guinness, Murphy's had breweries in almost all mid-size Irish towns, particularly those situated on a river. In the mid-1800s, with those convenient locations, it was a simple matter for the workers at Murphy's to load the barrels of stout onto a barge and take them where they were needed, up or down the river. To travel upstream, horses were harnessed to the barges. They plodded along the riverbanks, pulling the barges against the water's flow. To travel downstream, the river pilots guided the barges between the river banks. Transportation was not a problem.

The local breweries, along with the bacon factories, were usually the major employers in the Irish towns in the mid-1800s. The work was steady and clean, and it paid well enough. The breweries had one fringe benefit not offered at the bacon plant: while on the job, brewery employees could drink two pints of the creamy dark stout every day. Two pints. No more. The value of two pints added up if you were figuring total pay and, in the 1870s in Ireland, that little perk lured the steadiest, most dependable workers in town. Every brewery worker knew the rule. Two pints. No more.

John Francis Walsh, my great-grandfather, was a cooper, meaning he made barrels. From the fresh timbers cut in the nearby Tipperary forests, he trimmed, planed, and fitted each plank, before forging the shape of the steel rings that held the wooden staves together.

The barrels had to be leakproof and consistent in size so each would hold about the same number of ounces of the Murphy's products. The barrels had to be sturdy to withstand repeated fillings at the brewery, as well as the wear and tear of loading them onto and transporting them on the barges to the public houses up and down the rivers. They had to hold up under the abuse of sliding down the chutes to the basement storage of some public houses. They were heavy when full of Murphy's stout, and they were seldom handled gently, except when the publican or the Murphy's company man was around. Barrel-making was an art and it took years to become a journeyman cooper.

John Walsh knew his trade well. He had served his apprenticeship under the master hand of his brother-in-law and mentor, Patsy Jones, Clonmel's most respected cooper. The two had worked together for several years until Patsy felt that John was ready for the responsibility of making barrels for Murphy's, a company that demanded the best.

John had married Patsy's sister, Mary Ann, in November 1875, and like all good Catholic married couples, they were busy raising their growing family. They wasted no time adding to the household. They both wanted a big family as they had each grown up in one themselves.

Clear water of the River Suir rushes over the weir as it flows past Old Bridge House in Clonmel. Salmon and trout abound.

They lived with Mary Ann's parents in the family home in Old Bridge, a middle-class neighborhood. The family's house had two stories with several small bedrooms upstairs and a family area on the main floor. It was one of the oldest houses in the neighborhood, and was referred to as "Old Bridge House" by the nearby residents. It was located on a plot with a large garden in front, facing the River Suir, which separated Counties Tipperary and Waterford. The river split into two wide streams as it neared the Clonmel business area after flowing past Irishtown on the north side.

At Old Bridge, each of the two streams was about fifty feet wide, fast-flowing, and crystal clear—you could see trout and salmon almost any time of the year. After being divided for about three hundred feet, the two streams flowed back together along the quay, a street that paralleled the river. Both Murphy's and the bacon factory were located on the quay on the north side of the river in the middle of town. It was an easy walking distance for John from the house at Old Bridge to his cooper's work area at Murphy's.

Within ten months after the wedding, John and Mary Ann had their first child, Nicholas, named after John's father who lived in Dungarvan in County Waterford on the south Irish coast. After Nicholas was born, Margaret Mary came in nine short months; Mary Joanna (Janie) came fifteen months later; Michael Francis came two years later; and then Thomas, Patrick, Jack, another Margaret Mary[1], and Henry. When John was thirty-two and Mary Ann was thirty-four, they had been married twelve years, had eight surviving children, and buried Margaret Mary after she died of tuberculosis as a young child.

John, as did most of the lads he worked alongside, liked the stout. When he had the few coins to buy a pint in the pub at night, the cool, creamy Murphy's was the finishing touch to another day. The two pints he could drink at the brewery helped take him through the day until quitting time. Those two free pints at work hit the spot, even though there wasn't the same *craic* and music as at the pub.

John and the lads would occasionally stretch the free pints from two to three, sometimes four, and they were certain they were the only ones who knew that they had exceeded their limit. They were convinced there was no way Murphy's would miss a few extra pints and, besides that, the lads worked hard all day long—who would notice?

But one day, Murphy's did notice. John and several of the lads were caught red-handed and were given their pink slips.

---

1. It was an Irish custom to name a later child with the same first name as an earlier child who had died.

They were fired, canned, sacked, with no more free pints. And John had a wife and eight children at home. More than ten years on the job—all gone.

*   *   *   *

AFTER TWO MONTHS of searching for any job he could find, John got more bad news. One of the fired lads from the brewery overheard an employer say that Murphy's wanted to make examples of those they had sacked. Two pints were enough for any employee. Not three, two. Murphy's would not tolerate any employee drinking more than the limit. Not only would Murphy's not hire them back to the brewery they had been fired from, Murphy's would not hire them on at any other of their breweries up and down the rivers. Worst of all, John and the others who had been fired had been blacklisted—they would find no work at Murphy's, no work at Guinness, and no work at any of the small breweries anywhere in Ireland. That was one of the reasons that the brewers' association was organized—if a brewery employee broke the rules, the members of the association wanted to let the others know. There would be no work for the employee at any brewery.

The limit was two pints. No more. And suddenly no one else in Clonmel needed any barrels made.

*   *   *   *

JOANNA, MARY ANN'S younger sister, immigrated to St. Louis, Missouri, in the early-1880s. She was a determined, independent, single woman—she wanted to go to America, find a suitable Catholic husband, and raise her family in a place where there would be opportunity for all. She didn't want the same life as Mary Ann—constantly pregnant, scraping by with meager wages, and enduring those damp, cold, Irish winters which seemed to never end. She was in her early twenties.

With her limited savings and a small loan from her parents, Joanna rode the train from Clonmel to Thurles to Cork and sailed to America on the big boat from the harbor at Cobh. She passed through the immigrant reception building at Castle Gardens in New York, rode a train to St. Louis, and took a job as a domestic. She had had plenty of on-the-job training while she was living under her parents' roof—she could cook, she could sew, and she could keep house. She was well organized, and she was on her own. She was very brave to make that big move all alone.

Before long, Joanna met John King, an Englishman from Leeds, who worked as a machinist for the railroad in St. Louis. He was Catholic. His parents had both been born in Ireland. He had a good job, was a steady man, and would be a suitable husband for her and a good father for the family she wanted. They married in April 1887. By the following July, Joanna and John—still mourning the death of their first-born, a daughter who had died shortly after birth—had their second child on the way.

The letters from home told Joanna the story and plight of her sister, Mary Ann, who was still living in the house at Old Bridge, raising eight children, with a husband out of a job with no prospects. Despite John's loss of his job because of drinking, Joanna believed him to be a fine man, a good father, and good husband to her sister. She also missed her sister.

By October of that year, Mary Ann and John's youngest child, Henry, was old enough that his grandmother could take care of him for a period of time, so Mary Ann and John decided to accept John King's offer to bring themselves and one of the older children to St. Louis where they could begin a new life in the land of opportunity—where Murphy's had no breweries at all.

Castle Gardens, the Immigrant Reception Center in New York City, was later replaced by Ellis Island.

The three of them—John, Mary Ann, and Michael at age seven—began the long journey following the same route Joanna had taken to the States. They rode that train from Clonmel to Thurles to Cork, and sailed on the big boat from the harbor at Cobh to New York, after which they would pass through the lines of immigrants at Castle Gardens and then ride the train to St. Louis.

EVERYTHING SEEMED CHAOTIC at the immigrant reception house in New York: endless lines of people from everywhere, strange languages, strange odors, strange clothes. Bossy American officers in uniforms were yelling orders at everyone: "stay in line ... listen to what I say ... mothers and fathers, hold on to your children ... watch your baggage ... keep moving in line...."

It overwhelmed John and Mary Ann. It was a sight Michael and his parents had never seen, coupled with noises they had never heard. It was literally a whole new world.

The Irish pronounce the name Walsh like Welsh, so when the immigration officer wrote up little Michael's papers, the name became Welsh for the young lad because that's what it had sounded like to the officer. The name change happened without John and Mary Ann realizing it—their son had become Michael Welsh, and he would carry his new surname for the rest of his life. John and Mary Ann's surname was still Walsh, but their son's was Welsh.

$$* \quad * \quad * \quad *$$

MURPHY'S WAS BIG in Ireland. Guinness was big in Ireland. But in St. Louis, Anheuser-Busch was very big. They transported their beers up and down the rivers and across the plains, using all methods of transport.

Huge barges carried the barrels of lager up and down the Mississippi, up the Missouri, and up the Ohio—and along all the other rivers that flowed into them. Big, bulky dray wagons pulled by teams of huge horses carried Anheuser-Busch lager hundreds of miles over land.

America was moving west and so was Anheuser-Busch. They needed more and more barrels, and coopers were in short supply. With John King's guidance and his letter of recommendation, John Walsh went to work for Anheuser-Busch. As far as he knew, they did not offer two free pints. He had learned his lesson.

✳   ✳   ✳   ✳

LIVING WITH JOANNA and John King for almost one year and not having any rent expense, Mary Ann and John were able to save enough money to have their other seven children join them in St. Louis. With two grown cousins from their grandmother's Casey family to accompany them, the children took the same path as their family members—they rode the train from Clonmel to Thurles to Cork, sailed on the big boat from the harbor at Cobh, passed through the immigrant reception center at New York, and rode the train to St. Louis.

Mary Ann, John and Michael met the big group at the St. Louis train station. Years later, Marcelline's father, Thomas, recalled the large baskets of fruit that his parents were carrying when they all met at the station. He remembered—even though he was only four years old at the time—that when the big group had departed from Cobh, they had to take their food with them. Perishable fruits and vegetables had to be eaten within a couple of days at sea. Thomas said he couldn't eat enough bananas and oranges from the large baskets his parents had brought to the station.

On advice from Mary Ann, the two grown cousins accompanying the seven small children made certain that the paperwork at the immigration reception center listed the children's surnames as Welsh, like young Michael's. However, Mary's and my research showed that some of the children continued to use Walsh as their surname.

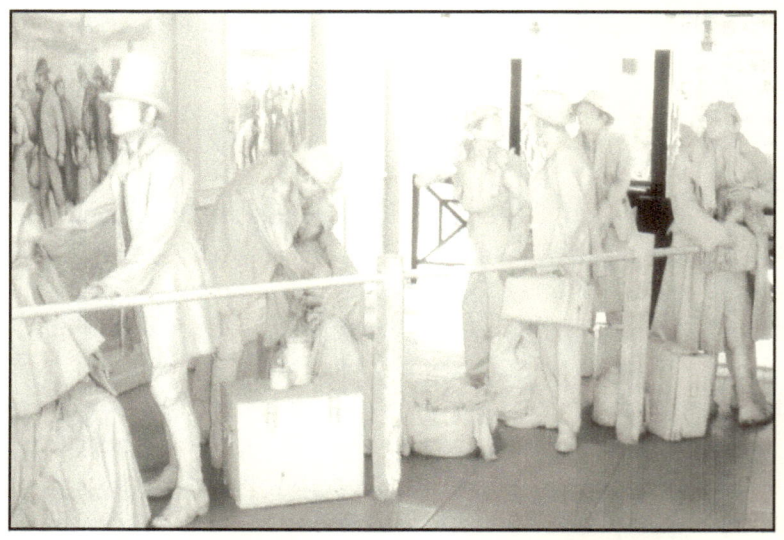

*A display in the Emigration Museum in Cobh represents
Irish departing for America or Canada in the 1800s.*

Soon enough, John and Mary Ann and the eight children were renting a house a few doors up the street from Joanna and John King, who were also raising their family and, like all good Irish and Leeds Catholics, were adding to it in rapid-fire order. In time, Joanna and John raised a total of five King children—they lost three others at birth.

*   *   *   *

THE YEARS BEFORE she and John emigrated had been turmoil for Mary Ann. She was the dutiful wife of an Irish cooper who had to endure the dismal day-to-day drudgery with a husband who was unemployable in her hometown. She had to depend upon her parents for housing and help with her children. She was the mother and shepherd of eight children, but she had to leave seven behind for over a year while she helped to establish a new home in America. She was also a mother overjoyed with having her flock under one roof as before, and she felt fulfilled as the wife of a reemployed cooper who had a good job working for a big American brewery.

But then something happened that she had not expected. She became pregnant.

Mary Ann managed throughout the difficult pregnancy with the help of her older children, but mainly with periodic help from Joanna, who had only recently moved from St. Louis to Hannibal, about one hundred miles north on the Mississippi River. John King had been transferred by the railroad, but Hannibal was close enough that Joanna could use her free pass and ride the train to St. Louis when Mary Ann was feeling poorly.

With John and their eight children crowded into the hospital waiting room, Mary Ann delivered twin boys and then died unexpectedly. The twins were stillborn. Mary Ann was still in her thirties.

John Francis Walsh, who had become so dependent upon Mary Ann for so many years in Ireland, and with whom he had been sharing a great new life in the States, was devastated. He was absolutely beside himself.

"What will I do now?" he asked himself.

The next day he packed his clothes, left all eight children with the nuns at the Sisters of St. Joseph Orphanage, and departed in the middle of the night. It took the nuns in St. Louis a couple of days to contact Joanna in Hannibal. With no other option, Joanna and John King took in and raised the deserted eight children, along with their own soon-to-be five children in Hannibal. Fittingly, Joanna was named Mother of the Year a few years later. Joanna and John King spent their final years in Hannibal as all the children grew up and made lives of their own.

*   *   *   *

WHILE COMPILING MY family's history, Mary and I could not verify events concerning my grandfather, Michael Welsh, from the time his mother died until he became a railroad engineer in Hannibal. The period from 1891 to about 1907 is a black hole in our records—one of the periods of time that was never recorded or remembered by other members of my family. We had only little tidbits of what occurred during that period stretching for about fifteen years.

Joanna and John King continued to raise their larger family and provided them with a Catholic education. Their daughter, Mary Margaret, became closely involved with a schoolmate, but their romance ended after her brother, Jimmy King, objected vociferously when the couple talked about marriage. Mary Margaret became depressed and despondent, joining the Order of the Sisters of St. Joseph in St. Louis and changing her name to Sister St. John, after her father.

Until her death many years later, Sister St. John kept the family that had remained in Ireland updated by exchanging letters with her cousin, Agnes Jones Powell, and later with Agnes' daughter, Betty Powell Kelly.

After John Walsh abandoned his eight children, he moved to Chicago, taking whatever jobs he could find. He drank heavily.

After several years he made contact with the family in Hannibal, offering to bring some of his children to Chicago to live with him, but the Kings understandably discouraged any such move because no mother or responsible adult would be there to assist in raising them.

When the eldest son, Nick Welsh, was nearly grown, he and two younger brothers, Patrick and Jack, did join their father. Within a short period of time, all three boys were diagnosed with advanced tuberculosis. Over a period of about two years, all three died and were buried back in Hannibal.

By 1907, Michael had reached the age of twenty-six and had gone to work for the same railroad as his Uncle John King to become an engineer. He drove short trains, carrying ore and other materials in and out of a cement manufacturing plant in Hannibal. It was a dusty, dirty place to work, and the fine particles from the plant and the smoke and coal dust from his switch engine contributed to the eventual breakdown of his health.

He married Nellie Gray, also of Hannibal, in 1907. Later that same year, my father, John Francis Welsh, was born. Another son, Thomas, was born in 1914, but he died at age three. Michael Francis Welsh Jr. was born in 1918. Finally, Robert Emmet Welsh was born in 1921.

Michael's father, John Walsh, moved back to Hannibal after Nick, Patrick, and Jack died of tuberculosis, and lived with his son, Thomas, and Thomas's wife, Nora, until Thomas was transferred to Montana by his company duPont. Then John moved in with Michael and Nellie. John died in Hannibal in 1915 at age sixty.

Michael's health began to fail soon after his father died, and he needed to get out of the cement plant atmosphere. He changed positions to become a railroad brakeman. But he soon fell seriously ill with tuberculosis, a disease that menaced many family members, killing his older sisters—Margaret Mary as a child and Mary Joanna (Janie) as a young mother—and three of his brothers.

A photo of the author's grandfather, Michael Welsh, taken before he was diagnosed with acute tuberculosis.

In those days, tuberculosis was one of the most feared ailments in the world. There were no preventative injections, no antibiotic, no known medical cure. Doctors could only recommend rest in a location at a high altitude with low humidity where it would be easier to breathe.

In 1923, his railroad brotherhood union paid all the expenses for Michael and his family to move from Hannibal to El Paso, Texas, widely reputed as a better climate for those suffering with tuberculosis. There were several tuberculosis sanatoriums in El Paso, primarily located on the foothills of Mount Franklin.

Michael was hospitalized in St. Joseph's Sanatorium. In addition to private rooms and large multi-patient wards, St. Joseph's had a large screened-in porch stretching the full length of the front of the building. Patients could get to the porch on their own or with the help of nurses and orderlies. The patients spent much of their time there, soaking in the dry, warm air and bright sunshine that gave them some relief and temporary comfort.

But the high altitude and dry climate came too late for Michael—he died in the sanatorium in 1924 at the age of only forty-three.

A spry, attractive Nellie Gray Welsh was all alone, with no immediate family to help her. When she and her husband had moved from Hannibal to El Paso, Nellie had left behind her brothers, Eugene, Oscar, and Gus, and her sisters, Mame and Edie. She was only forty-one years old, and her three sons were seventeen, seven, and three. It was up to her to head up the Texas family and make a living for all of them.

Time Capsule
1910 to 1930

America: The Titanic sinks off Newfoundland, claiming 1535 lives. The U.S. enters World War II, and before it ends, 1,400,000 Yanks fight in European trenches. Congress passes the Volstead Act, prohibiting the drinking of alcohol. The act drives the manufacturing, transportation, and sales of alcohol underground. The Nineteenth Amendment gives women the right to vote. The stock market crashes on Wall Street, and values drop to half. The Great Depression begins.

Ireland: The third Home Rule Bill passes, strongly opposed in Ulster. Irish volunteers march in Dublin, but they are ignored by British authorities, and they lack local support. Easter Rising is put down, some Irish leaders are jailed. Rebel leader Michael Collins signs a treaty with England, dividing six northern counties from the other twenty-six, angering Irish President de Valera. The treaty that splits Ireland leads to civil war. Collins dies in an ambush.

Family: Tuberculosis kills three of Michael Welsh's brothers in Chicago, and John Walsh returns to Hannibal where he dies in 1915. Suffering from failing health, Michael and his family move to arid El Paso, Texas, but the higher altitude and lower humidity fail to help, and he dies in 1924. John and Stene Welsh name their first son John Francis Welsh Jr., born in 1929. John King, Joanna's husband, dies in Hannibal in 1924.

CHAPTER FOUR

East 1442

BEFORE THERE WAS a Wal-Mart or a Sam's Club, before there were supermarkets or 7-Elevens, before there were big, striped parking lots or shopping carts, before there were TV dinners or even TV, before there were electronic scanners or plastic bags—before all that, there was Welsh's Food Store at 2432 Copper Street, El Paso, Texas; East 1442 by phone.

Welsh's Food Store was a mom-and-pop corner grocery—well, it was really a "mom" corner grocery because there was no "pop."

The proprietor was Nellie Gray Welsh. She had moved to El Paso from Hannibal, Missouri, in 1923 when Michael was stricken with tuberculosis. He spent several months in St. Joseph's Sanatorium, soaking in the sun when he wasn't coughing and spitting up phlegm and losing weight rapidly. He finally died in October 1924 at the early age of forty-three, leaving Nellie with $500 in life insurance money and three sons to raise.

So Nellie Gray Welsh bought a grocery store with the insurance money. A grocery store—lock, stock, and barrel—with fresh meat, fresh produce, fresh bread and milk, canned goods, paper products, candy, and soda pop. Nellie's grocery store occupied the ground floor of a two-story building at the corner of Copper and Kentucky streets. The building had a small apartment in the rear of the store and three apartments upstairs.

The store was located in the Highland Park neighborhood on the eastern slopes of El Paso's Mount Franklin. This closely-knit area contained mostly single-story, brick homes in a typical blue-collar neighborhood of the 1920s. The rocky mountainside kept the lawns to a minimum of grass and trees. The cost of water was high, but the neighborhood took pride in its appearance. If the grass was a little barren, at least the dirt was swept and the leaves raked. Whitewashed rocks formed borders for flowerbeds and were placed carefully around tree holes. There were rocking chairs and swings on the front porches. Some of the streets were paved, especially where the streetcar lines ran. The unpaved streets were dusty and rutted.

The paved streets served as playgrounds for the neighborhood kids who entertained themselves with baseball, touch football, kick the can, shinny, roller-skating, riding scooters made with two-by-fours and skate wheels, shooting rocks with slingshots, cutting strips from inner tubes for ammunition for their rubber guns, and riding old tires down the hills. Few kids had bicycles—they were too expensive.

The Highland Park streetcar ran from downtown El Paso to Cotton Street and then up the slope of the mountain, twisting and turning up the hill on the paved streets—right off Cotton to Erie Avenue, left on Ohio, right on Tremont Street to Indiana, right on Portland to Dakota, right on Copper Street, then up Kentucky to Louisville, right to Alabama Street and on up to Newman Park where the motorman switched the trolley, reversed the seat backs, moved his farebox and change dispenser from one end to the other before heading the streetcar back down the hill to the center of town.

As the Highland Park streetcar zigzagged its way toward the end of the line, it passed the San Antonio Grocery, the Tremont Grocery, and the Highland Park Grocery before it reached Welsh's Food Store—Nellie had all the competition she needed. Times were tough, but the Great Depression—when times would get even tougher—was still a few years away.

John, who was Nellie's oldest son at almost eighteen, was in his third year at El Paso High School. He felt he needed to quit school when his father died. John worked in the store some, helped watch after his brothers Mike (age seven) and Bobby (age three), and had a part-time job as a railroad callboy. He paged engineers, brakemen, firemen, conductors, and other crewmembers when their trains were about to begin their runs from the El Paso rail yards.

Nellie had a butcher, a clerk, and a couple of neighborhood kids to help her out in the store. She made a modest living, and the store's business was growing a little at a time.

*   *   *   *

GROCERY SHOPPING IN the 1920s was a day-to-day task for housewives. It wasn't something they dreaded. As a matter of fact, it was a social event, and women tried to get to the store early in the day. The fruits and vegetables were fresher and crisper, the bread had just been delivered freshly baked, and creamery-fresh milk had arrived only a few hours earlier.

At Welsh's Food Store, most purchases were made on credit. No one had invented credit cards yet. There were no food stamps or other welfare programs, although more people had less then. Practically no one paid with personal checks. A few paid cash.

Nellie kept a charge book for each customer. The top white copy went to the customer, and the yellow carbon copy stayed attached to the charge pad. When customers opened a credit account, they usually paid around the first or the fifteenth of the next month. Most payments came in about the tenth but a customer might skip a month if they were having a particular tough time. When that happened they did their best to catch up as quickly as they could because their credit standing was important—they wanted the convenience of shopping at a nearby store since they had to walk there and carry their purchases home.

By any standard, groceries were inexpensive. Shoppers could buy round steak for 20¢ per pound. Hamburger went three pounds for 25¢. Two cans of tomato sauce cost 7¢. Van Camp pork and beans were two for 9¢. Weekend specials included lettuce for a penny a head, fresh carrots and spinach for a penny a bunch, Armour hams for 22¢ a pound, and two rolls of Zee or Waldorf toilet tissue for 7¢. Yes, groceries were cheap, but wages were low. Jobs were difficult to find, and unemployment was high.

The suppliers of Welsh's Food Store extended credit on much the same basis as Nellie: buy from us, pay on time, and you will be a preferred customer; buy from us, pay when you can, and you will be a good customer. It was important to Nellie that her customers pay promptly because there was never a large surplus of cash in her deposit and checking account at The State National Bank in downtown El Paso.

The charge pads were kept in a metal cabinet under the counter at the front of the store. They were arranged alphabetically with each customer's name printed on the top of the pad. Balances were totaled up each month and written on a ledger card that was kept in another metal cabinet. Generally, accounts were settled up each month with a payment in full but, if a customer was behind, Nellie would accept a partial payment because she knew that her customers were trying to do the right thing. And besides, most customers were Nellie's friends.

*   *   *   *

BEING A SINGLE mom and a storeowner wasn't easy. Nellie had to wake up very early each morning, fix and pack Mike's lunch, and then get him on his way to school. A daytime maid from Juárez arrived early to watch after Bobby and do other chores at the apartment. The store opened after Mike left for school each weekday at about 7:30 a.m., but groceries were being sold and business was underway long before then.

The Surebest, Purity, and Kahn's Bakery route men dropped off boxes of fresh bread and pastries and stacked them on the front sidewalk near the store door at about 4:00 a.m. They estimated the store's needs based on the elementary inventory sheets they kept. After the route man dropped off all his full boxes from his step van, he would eat breakfast and then double back to adjust the quantities he had left, check in his order, take out any old bread he knew wouldn't sell, and restock his space on the bread rack. In the afternoon on his way home, he stopped by his larger stores to straighten up the portion of the bread shelf where he displayed his items. The salesman who did the best job got the best location on the sales rack—and that meant more sales.

Nellie Gray Welsh and her two youngest sons, Mike Jr. (left) and Bob, in about 1925.

It worked the same way with milk, except there were four dairies competing for Nellie's business. They didn't drop their products off on the sidewalk as early as the bakeries, but they were there at about the time the store opened. And, then, there was the problem of empty milk bottles.

A large number of Nellie's customers had their milk delivered to their front door each morning. They left their empty bottles on the porch at night, usually with a note telling the home-delivery salesman what to leave—a quart of homogenized, or a half-pint of table cream, maybe a quarter-pound stick of butter. The home-delivery salesman came by the house at the end of the week to collect.

But some of Nellie's customers didn't like that system, so they bought their dairy items from the store where it might cost a few cents less than home delivery. When they bought from the store, they had to return their empty bottles. Those bottles had to be placed into milk crates for the store route salesman to pick up. Often, the customer failed to rinse out the empty bottles, and they smelled bad. Unwashed bottles could cause a roach problem in the store. To avoid that, the empties were kept isolated in the storage area of the store and were usually rinsed out by a store clerk during the day.

The soft drink route men, representing about eight or nine different brands, came twice a week to fill up their space on the store shelves. Only the salesman who furnished the cold soda case came more often. At Welsh's Food Store, that was usually the Coca-Cola man.

The Coca-Cola man, wearing a spotless, freshly starched white uniform with thin green stripes, came every day soon after the store opened. He filled the case with freshly-chipped ice every morning, drained the cold water from yesterday's ice, emptied the metal caps receptacle from the case, and kept the case clean, dry, and shiny on the outside. In exchange, he had plenty of his items in the case in the most convenient locations. He agreed to keep a few of his competitor's bottles in the cold soda case and he had to do a good job because the Pepsi, 7UP, Barq's, Dr. Pepper, RC, Nehi, and Grapette salesmen all wanted his space and they had plenty of cold soda cases to replace his if they got the chance.

EVERY NIGHT WHEN the store closed at 6:00 p.m., Nellie made her order for the next morning's produce deliveries. Because she was a single mom with her chores to do at home before the store opened, and because she didn't have an experienced assistant who could go to the city market and personally select each day's produce, Nellie had to rely on two produce wholesalers to select the best items they had available and deliver them to the store before 8:00 a.m.

Certain produce houses had a policy of handling only the best grades on the market, even though their prices were a little higher. These suppliers usually had the business of the top restaurants. Other suppliers featured the next to the top grades, were usually a little cheaper, and normally had the schools' business. Nellie's favored supplier was Crombie Co. because their bananas were the best, their tomatoes were usually at just the right point of ripening, and their potatoes were the freshest and most uniform in size. They also hand-bagged the five-pound mesh sacks so there were no rotten or bruised potatoes in the bag.

The other produce items Nellie needed were usually the same quality at the other wholesalers, so she bought them wherever the price was best and the delivery dependable.

Nellie's store clerk was also the produce manager. The highly perishable items were removed from the produce display cases every night at closing, and placed in a walk-in cooler in the rear storage area of the store. Next morning when the deliveries arrived, he would wash, trim if necessary, and place the new products in the case, and stack the carry-over from the day before on top after he re-worked it. He was making sure that all the produce was good quality, not bruised or overly squeezed.

Nellie wanted her produce to be the best of the produce sold at any store along the streetcar line.

After the produce display cases were filled, the clerk manually turned on a cold water mist-spray in the section of the department where he had placed the vegetable items needing regular moistening. Of course the moistening added to the shelf life of each unit but, equally important, the dew-like mist brightened the coloring of the vegetables and made them more appealing to those early shoppers. Periodically through the day, the clerk misted the vegetables on the case to keep them fresh—it only took him a couple of minutes. He also stocked and dusted the grocery shelves. One part-time neighborhood boy usually worked a few hours during the day, and on busy weekends, Nellie occasionally brought in another youngster to help where needed.

＊   ＊   ＊   ＊

THERE WAS ONE problem that was potentially bigger than slow-paying customers: butchers. It seemed all good butchers drank. And no butcher showed up on time every day every week—at least not sober.

A good butcher kept his product fresh and sanitary. He kept his refrigerated case at the correct temperature, and each product he pre-trimmed or pre-ground was placed on clean waxed paper atop a stainless steel platter, and was arranged attractively in stacks or piles. The artificial greenery that separated each item had to be clean. The case top and front glass had to be spotless. His butcher-block had to be scraped and sanitized throughout the day. His knives had to be sharp and clean and in place on the knife rack. His cooler had to be cold and organized and the meat hooks had to be sanitary. The sawdust on the floor that caught the scraps had to be raked regularly, added to daily, and completely changed out at least every few days. Chickens had to be washed upon receipt, and the ice they were shipped in had to be rinsed and drained away to prevent odors. His slicer, his handsaw, and his grinder had to be clean and sharp at all times. He had to order products from meat salesmen, check in their deliveries, and still make a profit.

Keeping up with all this for nine to ten hours a day, six days a week, and—on top of all that—having to wait on customers (not all of whom were pleasant themselves) with a cheery smile and a how-are-you-today-Mrs.-Customer attitude all the time—all that—was more than most butchers could handle. So, they drank. Some, drank a lot.

Nellie was like every other grocer—she babied a good butcher. If he missed a day, she was angry and let him know it, but she usually forgave him because she knew the next one would do the same thing. Sometimes, enough was enough, and first chance she had, she made a change. Butchers were an ongoing nightmare.

*   *   *   *

BY SEPTEMBER 1926, John had quit high school, married his sweetheart Ernestyne, and gone to work for Swift & Co., the big meatpacker. When his dad died, John wanted to earn money to help his mother as she started her grocery store. John was a serious but outgoing young man who wanted to get ahead. He started out working in the coolers at Swift, hoisting beef quarters and pork sides, rotating merchandise, selecting and loading orders for customers and, thereby, serving his apprenticeship learning the meat business. It wasn't a bad job—the hours were from very early morning to mid-afternoon, the coolers were chilly but tolerable, if you wore a cooler coat. The pay was good enough that he and Ernestyne had their own apartment. Ernestyne was a part-time salesclerk at a ladies' dress shop downtown, where her pay supplemented John's salary.

Soon John's apprenticeship ended and he went on the road in a company roadster, traveling southern New Mexico to sell Swift products to grocers and cafés along the two-lane highways stretching from Las Cruces to Deming to Lordsburg to Silver City to Hatch and over the mountains to Carrizozo. When she was not working, Ernestyne accompanied John on his route. She read and knitted and visited with the grocers' wives. John was almost twenty and Ernestyne was almost seventeen. The young couple had a pretty good life.

As time passed into the late-1920s, the "good" butcher at his widowed mother's store worried John. He noticed the good butcher's ways around Nellie—the extra attention, the admiring looks, the interest in the rest of the store that other butchers never showed—and John didn't like it. So after lots of thought and with almost four years of training at Swift & Co., John turned in his roadster and resigned his job in June of 1930. He went to work for his mom in what was now the family business.

*   *   *   *

JOHN BECAME THE butcher for Nellie's store and gradually became more involved in management with his mother. Sales had continued to increase at a steady pace, and John convinced Nellie that free delivery would bring even more dollars of sales to Welsh's Food Store. So she bought a shiny, red Chevy panel truck with a single seat, and lots of space to stack orders. The lettering on its sides read: "Welsh's Food Store. 2432 Copper Street. El Paso, Texas. Free Delivery. Phone East 1442."

Ernestyne, known as Stene, became the order solicitor and the order taker for the store, and she worked every day without pay because John's wage was adequate. Besides that, it was all that Welsh's Food Store could afford.

Stene started by telephoning all the occasional customers and offering free delivery and charge account privileges. She began setting up a regular delivery schedule. Soon, other customers saw the shiny red Chevy panel truck advertising free delivery, and some wanted in on that service. It was easy: Stene called the customer, or the customer called Stene. Phone East 1442.

This one-on-one telephone conversation was a wonderful opportunity for Stene to sell items not on the customer's want list. She could mention how fresh the Kentucky Wonder green beans were this morning, and how the meat market had made a great buy on smoked picnic hams that looked to be very lean and were only 14¢ a pound that day, or that the frying chickens looked particularly plump and juicy that morning.

After Stene finished taking an order, she passed it along to the clerk, who gathered the items for the order from the shelves, stacked them in a delivery box, and placed the perishable items together in the storage cooler where they stayed until the delivery truck was ready to load. Each order was collected, the prices added up on the cash register, and the total amount due was then recorded on the charge pad or set up for collection if it was a cash order. Orders were arranged in delivery sequence, loaded on the shiny, red Chevy panel truck, and off the clerk went with the morning deliveries. The same procedure took place again after lunch because some customers wanted their deliveries closer to the evening meal.

John had been correct: free delivery picked up sales. The phone line was busy at East 1442.

*   *   *   *

A FEW MONTHS after John had started at the store, Nellie bought a two-bedroom stucco house across the street from Welsh's, and John and Stene moved into her old apartment in the rear of the store. Over time, Nellie had expanded the store by moving the storage area back, eliminating the living room and a closet from the apartment. The big kitchen had been turned into a sitting room with its couch and overstuffed chair and radio, a dining space with a leaf table and four chairs, and a kitchen in the corner. The apartment also had a fair-size bedroom and closet, an enclosed back porch, and a bathroom. The entrance and exit from the apartment was either through the store's storage area or through a side door and down about ten wooden steps onto a rocky vacant lot next to the store.

In December 1929, some three years after their wedding and about six months before John left Swift & Co., Stene delivered a son whom they named John Francis Welsh Jr., thereby unceremoniously ending a custom that had been followed by the Irish family for generations. The custom called for the first son to be named after the father's father, the second son to be named after the mother's father, the third son to be named after the father, and the fourth son to be named after an Irish hero. Any daughter could be named whatever the parents chose. Either the children's first or middle name had to be after a Catholic saint, such as St. Francis or St. Mary. John and Stene had no plans for that many children, so why bother about the custom? The first son was John Francis Welsh Jr., or Little Johnny.

Stene Welsh

John F. Welsh Sr.

After a few months in a wicker crib next to his parents' bed, Little Johnny was moved onto the back porch during the night-time and then, during the day when he was a little bigger, into a canvas swing that hung from a chain and spring attached to a hook in the ceiling above the center aisle of the store. Stene could keep her eyes on the baby from her counter at the front, and customers *ooohed* and *aahhed,* tickling and playing with the baby during the time he wasn't asleep.

*   *   *   *

TIME PASSED INTO the 1930s, and the business prospered. Nellie's two younger sons, Mike and Bobby, were progressing through high school and grade school. They both worked occa-sionally in the store, but they earned spending money by mowing lawns, sweeping porches, painting fences or doing any other odd jobs they could find.

The neighborhood changed little. During the Great Depression, Highland Park, the blue-collar area, suffered along with most other parts of El Paso. Some men were laid off from work and took odd jobs where they could be found. Others worked for the city or big companies, where lay offs where not as common. Few women worked. Yet some families were fortunate when both the husband and wife were working because they could afford to hire daymaids who lived in Juárez, Mexico. The daymaids took the streetcar to and from work every day. They cleaned the house inside and out, washed clothes in washtubs that were heated by a wood fire usually set in the backyard, dried clothes on a wire or rope clothesline, did some cooking, and watched the kids, if there were any. Maids were usually paid $5 a week plus streetcar fare—another 50¢ a week. The U.S. Immigration Service overlooked this practice. Times were hard during the Great Depression, but everyone adjusted and made do with what they had.

Payments on charge accounts were slow. But payments of some amount were made. Fortunately, Welsh's Food Store had very few bad debts.

Delivery was flourishing, however. Deliveries to customers within a few blocks of the store were made by bicycle. Clerks or part-time neighborhood lads, who worked after school, made the bike deliveries. They simply cut thumbholes at the bottom on the side of a cardboard box, loaded the order into the box, and held the box with their thumbs while holding onto the handlebars, steering with four fingers and their palms. It took an accident or two pumping up the rocky streets on the mountainside before the delivery lads caught on, but it was faster service to customers, and it saved the cost of gasoline and other truck expenses.

Customers knew most of the delivery boys and learned to trust them, almost without exception. Delivery boys were instructed to take the order to the back door, knock on the screen door, and place each item of the order onto the kitchen table once the door was opened. Some customers asked the delivery boys to place the cold items into the icebox. Customers signed the delivery/charge account slip and the delivery boy hustled back to the store. No tipping was allowed. It was free delivery. Phone East 1442.

*   *   *   *

NELLIE GRAY WELSH'S health began to slip in the mid-1930s, even to the point that she spent very little time in the store. She was in the first stages of a neurological malady later called Parkinson's disease. A steady shaking started in her hands and then moved to her wrist and forearm, then to her entire arm and shoulder. Her head was next. It was not a violent shaking, just a trembling at first, but it seemed as if it never stopped. She was not an invalid at the start; she could continue to do things about the house and could still hold the cards at her semi-weekly bridge games, but she couldn't drive, and she had to be very careful when walking. Soon, she used a cane.

John ran the store. He did all the book work and met with the salesmen such as the Red & White wholesaler who called on the store twice a week for his grocery order. Sales continued to grow and more clerks were added full-time or part-time.

When the wholesaler's delivery arrived each week, every employee pitched in to put the individual items onto the shelves and mark the retail price with a black Listo grease pencil. When that was finished, the employees rebagged pinto beans and rice from hundred-pound burlap sacks into two- and five-pound paper bags. Pintos and rice were popular—they were filling and inexpensive.

In early-1935, Stene became pregnant again. But, several months into the pregnancy, her doctor could not detect any heartbeat and prepared Stene for a stillbirth. She could not feel any movement from the baby, so she made no preparation for her second child—no new diapers, no baby showers, no new baby clothes, no new crib or blankets, no baby bottles.

The delivery plan was easy: when the time came, John and Stene would drop off Little Johnny at Nellie's house, drive about ten blocks to Masonic Hospital where they would meet the doctor and await the delivery. She would be in the hospital two or three days to recover. There was no need to be there long enough for the baby to get strong enough to leave, because that was not a factor.

The delivery plan went off as expected on November 11, 1935—except for one detail: the expected stillborn child arrived alive and well, kicking and hollering, boasting of his five-pound, five-ounce frame. Hurriedly, gratefully, and happily, a name was chosen. John and Stene's new son would be Richard (after no one in particular) Ernest (after Stene's father). Again, the name followed no Irish custom, came from no Irish saint, and certainly didn't come from an Irish hero.

Dick was born on Armistice Day, but it was just another day at Welsh's Food Store—good service to the customers, clerks made Stene's calls for customers' orders and took called in orders. It was still free delivery. Phone East 1442.

IN LESS THAN two years, John and Stene ran out of living space with Little Johnny and baby Dick, so they moved into their first home. It had two bedrooms, separate living and dining rooms, a kitchen, and a garage at the rear. The rooms were larger than the cramped apartment had been, and the best thing was that it was located on Federal Street, only one block from the store.

Stene hired Maria Delgado, a day-maid who lived in El Paso rather than Juárez, and who would be able to ride the streetcar to and from work every day but Sunday. Maria became a regular part of the Welsh family for the next ten years until her health failed and she passed away. During those years, she refused to learn how to operate an automatic washing machine, although she did accept the wringer attachment that she used with her washtub heated by a wood fire in the backyard. Clotheslines were good enough for Maria. In those ten years, she did appreciate the switch from streetcars to busses which weren't so noisy. And the busses had no cane-backed chairs.

*   *   *   *

WHEN SELECTIVE SERVICE began prior to World War II, the employee market shrank to practically nothing. Able-bodied young men who were dependable, honest clerks or delivery boys—even butchers—were gobbled up for military service when their draft numbers came up. And that included both of Nellie's youngest sons Mike and Bobby, although it took three different physical exams before Mike would be drafted because doctors continued to find spots on his lungs when they viewed his chest X-rays. Finally, when it became harder and harder for the draft board to fill monthly quotas, Mike was inducted.

He had been a post office special delivery mailman riding a motorcycle, so the Army assigned him to a motorized cavalry unit that led military convoys across the country. After a short time, however, his unit was shipped to Panama where the high-humidity climate caused the spots on his lungs to develop into active tuberculosis. Bobby, then an employee of the Southern Pacific railroad, was inducted at the same time as his brother and was assigned to a railroad battalion that handled equipment transportation both in the U.S. and later in Africa and Italy. So Mike and Bobby were no longer available to work in Welsh's Food Store.

While other male employees seemed virtually unavailable, John struck pay dirt when he landed H. L. McCracken, an older, experienced butcher with only a minor drinking habit. "Old Man Mac," as he was called, moved into a second-floor apartment above the store with his wife and two teenaged daughters.

By then, John had been the produce buyer for several years along with everything else. Three days a week, he got up at 4:00 a.m., drove to the city market and hand-selected all the fruits and vegetables, had each produce wholesaler load them on the Chevy truck, and drove the produce back to the store where the order was then worked as always, sometimes by female clerks. This was an ongoing chore that John did not relish, but it was important to the success of the store. Besides, delivery by the produce wholesalers was no longer dependable since they were also experiencing problems obtaining enough gasoline for their trucks, and hiring and keeping employees because of the war.

One morning at about 6:30 a.m., when John arrived back at the store from picking up the produce, he noticed a healthy, well-dressed, young man in his twenties standing by the front door of the store. He introduced himself as Manny Alvarado. He said he had worked for a grocer acquaintance of John's, named Mike Caldarella, who had been forced to close his store when he was drafted. Mike had told Manny that he knew John Welsh needed a head clerk who was experienced in all areas of the store, and suggested he call John for a job. Manny was classified 4-F (unfit for military service for health reasons) because his eyesight was bad. He was able to drive a car, but only barely. Manny was married, had one child, and was looking for steady work. John was thrilled, Manny was hired, and together they unloaded the produce order right then. Their relationship began in 1941 and lasted until 1946 when Manny's original employer, Mike Caldarella, reopened his store after being released from active military service. The relationship began again in 1954 when Mike sold his store and Manny was rehired at Welsh's. The relationship continued for more than twenty years.

Manny was licensed to drive, but he could barely see. Additionally, gasoline was rationed during the war, but Manny still made all those free deliveries in the same Chevy truck, and orders still flowed over the phone at East 1442.

*   *   *   *

SHOPPING FOR GROCERIES was different during World War II. All products were in short supply, if they were available at all. There were price controls that grocers had to follow and display in a price catalogue in the store. Many scarce food products were rationed. The federal government issued ration coupons monthly that were presented to the grocer by a customer when a product was purchased. Rationing not only helped by reducing the sales of scarce items—it prevented consumers from hoarding certain products.

American farm labor was also in very short supply, and farm products were shipped to the military before they became available to the general public. Grocers turned in the ration coupons to wholesalers when replacement products were purchased.

The selection of products was limited. There were only a few cleaning products. Detergents were unheard of—housewives washed clothes with bar soaps, scrubbing the clothes over washboards propped against the side of washtubs. Only dainty materials were washed differently—housewives generally used Ivory Flakes for their delicate underwear. Ammonia and bleach were the cleaning products of choice. There were no dishwashing liquids, fabric softeners, deodorizers, sponges, paper towels, glass cleaners, paper napkins, insecticides, sponge mops—they had not been invented or discovered yet. Hot water was a valuable commodity because of limited electricity and natural gas, so showers were short. It was not quite a weekly bath situation, but it came close.

Meat was very limited. What beef, pork and poultry were produced went to fill military needs first. Many meatpackers had to close because of supply of product and labor. Grocers depended on long-standing relationships with the remaining packers, hoping to receive some fresh products when the delivery truck arrived each week. A store might receive a front quarter of beef one week and perhaps a hindquarter the next week; a slab of bacon, a pork loin, several pork shoulders or hams, and a wooden crate of two dozen chickens packed in ice might be on the truck—that was the hope of the grocers.

There was little waste in the meat markets. Butchers carefully trimmed the fat away from beef and pork cuts, and even some of the suet was used to make pinwheels or added to ground meat to stretch it out. A pinwheel resembled a slice of a jellyroll and was made by rolling a round or flank steak around a slice of white trimmed fat. Pinwheels were sliced less than an inch thick and were held together with a wooden skewer.

Housewives added cracker meal or bread crumbs to ground meat to make meatloaf. Butchers made mock chicken legs by blending ground beef and cracker meal and wrapping it around a skewer. Surplus fat from the meat market trimmings was sold to rendering plants where it was converted into lard for cooking.

The shortage of meat was a constant problem at Welsh's Food Store. About once a month when the store was closed on Sunday, John and his butcher, Old Man Mac, would drive through the farming areas north and south of El Paso, stopping to talk to farmers about purchasing a cow or a calf or a hog. Sometimes this paid off and arrangements would be made for a small packer or locker plant to pick up the animal from the farm, slaughter it, and dress it out for Welsh's Food Store. The cost was not important; the availability was.

When fresh beef or pork or poultry was available in the meat market at Welsh's Food Store, word spread through the Highland Park neighborhood like a wildfire. But, upon strict instructions from John, Old Man Mac developed his own rationing program. Regular customers always got something—almost certainly in limited amount, but they got some fresh meat. Still Old Man Mac always had an eye on the future, so he tried to accommodate strangers with something that they could probably not find elsewhere.

Some lunchmeats were usually available. Bologna and pickle pimiento loaf and spiced luncheon loaf (a spam-like product) might be in the meat case on the weekend. Cheese was rationed and no imitation cheese products had been developed at that time—only round hoops or loaves of cheese, such as mild cheddar or Colby or American, which were cut in the meat market, might be available.

Rationing helped control the supply of most grocery products. Housewives did a lot of baking with regular enriched flour and cornmeal because mixes were not available. They made a lot of bread and rolls and cornbread. Soup was a common main course since cabbage, celery, tomatoes, and onions were usually in the produce case. Fruit was limited to apples that were grown nearby. Occasionally oranges and grapefruit were available, and Welsh's Food Store might be lucky some mornings to find stalks of bananas at the produce wholesalers. The bananas might be ripe or fully green, but it didn't matter because bananas were hard to get.

Welsh's Food Store in El Paso's Highland Park circa 1948.

The owner of the Red & White wholesaler, James A. Dick, had been in business in El Paso for many years. Mr. Dick had helped Nellie during the tough early years of her business and she had reciprocated by being a loyal customer, always paying for her invoices as quickly as she could. Mr. Dick always treated Nellie as a special customer and, on one memorable occasion, had shipped one hundred cases of large cans of some obscure fruit juice to the store without any preapproval. Approval did not matter. The juice was not a rationed item, and it was tasty and reasonable in price. Neighbors saw the wholesaler's truck unloading stacks of the juice, and they started flocking in to see just what product Welsh's Food Store had received in such a huge amount.

One hundred cases of anything was a lot for Welsh's Food Store. There wasn't enough room in the store for the truck driver to stack the cases, but John, Manny, and Old Man Mac hauled most of it to Nellie's garage across the street. Old Man Mac's rationing system was put to use again, but the entire hundred cases—1,200 cans—were gone in two days, and it took that long because much of it had to be hauled from Nellie's garage back to the store. Manny talked about that episode for years.

*   *   *   *

MIKE WELSH WAS medically discharged from the Army in early 1943 after spending nearly two years in military hospitals recovering from tuberculosis. He had gone from a healthy 190 pounds down to under one hundred pounds and was almost skeleton-like. But the location of hospitals in Denver and Fort Bayard, New Mexico—both at high altitudes—helped to arrest his tuberculosis, and he was sent home to recuperate. In due time, Mike improved to the point where his own recuperation program went into effect: sleep late, play golf in the early afternoon every day, and go to the bars in Juárez every night. He was single, and he lived at home with his mother. His new lifestyle did not please her, and she ordered him to work in the store at least some of the time. John and Stene, who had been working twelve or more hours a day, six days a week, for a long time, readily accepted him. The addition of Mike to the payroll also increased the size of management of the family business.

*   *   *   *

BOBBY WELSH SPENT almost four years in North Africa and Italy as the war wound down. He had married Lila Brookins, a Floridian transplanted to El Paso, just before he had been drafted. Lila lived with Nellie much of the time during the war years and worked in the grocery store from time to time. When Bobby returned to El Paso after being discharged, he got a salesman's job at Kraft Foods, and he and Lila moved into a small apartment not too far from the Highland Park neighborhood where he had grown up.

Although Bob had not worked in the store much as a youngster, he had been around the grocery business since the day Nellie had bought the store. So his job at Kraft suited him well because he sold products to grocers, placed them on the stores' shelves, and took care of damaged and spoiled products. He was exposed to the ways that other grocers operated. He saw opportunities for independent grocers ahead, and that made him wish he was involved in the family business. But Welsh's Food Store could not afford another family man, even though Manny had returned to his former employer.

Then things changed for everyone in 1946 when Welsh's Food Store got an opportunity to open a second store in the Ascarate neighborhood in El Paso's Lower Valley.

*   *   *   *

THROUGH THE CLOSE relationship between Welsh's Food Store and the Red & White wholesaler, John was offered the store location that had the possibility of larger sales because it was a bigger building on a heavily traveled highway. There were other retail businesses nearby which would likely add to the sales potential by bringing extra traffic, and Nellie agreed that it was an opportunity they should not let pass them by.

This new venture, and her declining health, prompted Nellie to reorganize the family business. But there were complications: she had three sons, equal in her eyes, working for the store. Still John had been involved in operation of the business for twenty years. After discussions with her three sons and her accountant, Nellie decided to give the business to the three sons in an equal partnership with Mike and Bob making monthly payments from their own resources to John to compensate him for his twenty years of service. It was understood that John would be the boss because of his experience and age.

Nellie's financial needs would be met from the profits of the business, but her Parkinson's disease forced her placement into a nursing home when she became bedridden. She died in 1954.

With the ownership problem resolved, Welsh's Food Store had sufficient management to begin a partnership that would last another sixteen years until 1962 when John bought out

Mike's and Bob's interest. Both of his brothers had grown weary of the ultra-competitive grocery business in post-war El Paso. During those sixteen years, the family business took many twists and turns. Through banking friends, Welsh's Food Store was offered a new location, and the Ascarate store was replaced with El Paso's first real supermarket located in a new, large, strip shopping center on the Fort Bliss military reservation. It became the first Welsh's Supermarket. The original Welsh's Food Store on Copper Street closed in 1955 and was replaced with another large supermarket two blocks away on Alabama Street, which was by then a busy north-south thoroughfare. A third super-market was opened in 1960 in a new, fast-growing housing area in East El Paso, replacing the Fort Bliss store when the federal government cancelled its lease. Another supermarket was opened in 1965 in Central El Paso. John and Stene's son, John Jr. (the author), joined the business in 1953, and Dick joined in 1955.

The family business' name had changed from Welsh's Food Store to Welsh's Supermarkets, and it became El Paso's leading independently owned supermarket company. It was soon the target for larger chains to buyout because of store locations, rep-utation, and volume of sales. With John slipping into poor health, preventing further expansion, and the buyout offers intensifying from competing chains, John Jr. left the family business in 1966 for food wholesaling, and Dick left in 1973, also for wholesaling. John sold the Central El Paso store on Per-shing Drive in 1968, the East El Paso store on McRae Boule-vard in 1973. The Alabama Street store—in the neighborhood where it all began—was sold a month after John died in January 1974. Stene, stricken with throat cancer in 1969, died in April 1975.

The last customer was served at Welsh's one month after John's death in 1974—almost fifty years after Nellie had opened her corner grocery on the streetcar line in Highland Park. The end had come for East 1442.

Time Capsule
1930 to 1940

America: The Great Depression cuts the national income by 50 percent, 5500 banks become insolvent, and unemployment hits 25 percent. Franklin Roosevelt and the democrats sweep Herbert Hoover and the republicans from office, pledging the New Deal for all Americans. New programs put many back to work and the economy improves. A drought devastates the Midwest. Congress passes the Social Security Act and the National Neutrality Act, however the U.S. girds for war.

Ireland: De Valera and his *Fianna Fail*, the warriors of Ireland, are elected to power, but he refuses to take the oath that requires "faithfulness" to British royalty. Eventually, a compromise puts *Fianna Fail* in control of the Irish Parliament. A constitution declaring the State of "Eire" is approved in 1937. An agreement ends the economic war with England. The English give up naval and military rights to Irish ports as part of the 1921 treaty. The IRA gains strength.

Family: Agnes and George Powell raise five children in Old Bridge House in Clonmel. The $500 insurance money from Nellie Gray's husband's death is used to buy a grocery store. John and Stene Welsh raise two sons and work long hours to build business in Nellie's El Paso store despite hard economic times. Free delivery service is offered to customers, and the grocery's business increases. Doctors treat the founder Nellie Welsh for the malady that is now called Parkinson's disease. Joanna Jones King dies in 1936 in Hannibal at age seventy-six.

CHAPTER FIVE

Back and Forth

BY THE SUMMER of 1995, Mary and I had made several trips back to Ireland, and we had confined our annual vacations to flights between Texas and Shannon, the arrival airport for flights across the Atlantic to Ireland. The cost of each trip was such that we tried to schedule one every eighteen months or so because it would take us about that long to accumulate enough frequent flyer miles to pay for at least one economy round-trip seat. We would make one trip in the springtime, and the next the following fall; we would use the time between trips to determine the length of the next trip, where we would stay, and pick out any section of the country we might want to visit. It was a lot of fun just planning each trip.

After that first trip in 1988, when we had stayed at different bed and breakfasts and small hotels, we decided it would be better for us to locate near Clonmel since we would be spending most of the time with the relatives or on golf courses nearby. For our needs it was centrally located and almost any section of Ireland was within an easy drive from Clonmel.

In 1989, we spent about a month at Mrs. Margaret Whelan's bed and breakfast up the street from the Kelly's house—at a daily cost of about $30 for both of us. That was the trip during which we were given the Mayor's Reception.

Mrs. Whelan, being a neighbor and well acquainted with Betty Kelly, took special care of us. We had the best of the four rooms she rented out daily—it was the one that was painted pink with flowery pink wallpaper and that had a large *en suite* bathroom and an instant hot water heater on the shower wall.

Mrs. Whelan's huge Irish breakfast consisted of eggs cooked our way, hot tomato wedges, fried rashers (lean bacon), fresh orange juice, coffee or tea, hot oatmeal or cereal and milk, and brown bread freshly toasted and ready to be topped with a scoop of creamy Irish butter.

It was a breakfast that filled you up for hours, so we made a habit of eating at about 8:30 a.m., and then enjoying an early evening meal at one of Clonmel's diverse restaurants, unless we had special plans for that night. This schedule allowed us plenty of time during the day for whatever we had scheduled, whether it was shopping in downtown Clonmel, playing eighteen holes of golf at the Clonmel Golf Club, visiting the relatives, or taking the short drive to the south coast in County Waterford and enjoying the views of the Celtic Sea crashing into the rocky shores at least a hundred feet below the twisty two-lane highway. (I think that is one of Ireland's most spectacular views and the spot where my dream ocean view home would be located.)

Mrs. Whelan's home was close enough to the downtown district for us to walk there often, weather permitting. It was a fun month at Mrs. Whelan's, except that we had to live out of our suitcases and had to take our laundry to a shop downtown. And since the price of the daily breakfast was included in the $30 rate, the only extra expense we had was for the evening meal and our entertainment at the pub every night—we seldom missed out on the *craic* at Eldon's.

The south coast of Ireland near Annestown, County Waterford.

A day at the beach at Dunmore East, County Waterford.

BEFORE LEAVING FOR that second trip, Mary had thought it would be a good idea to expose the Irish kinfolk to her version of Mexican food, particularly since they had been so receptive to us when we all met on our first trip. Mary knew that virtually none of the ingredients or products she would need for the fiesta feast would be available in the Clonmel supermarkets, so she figured out the menu and started gathering everything she would need to take with us on the Delta flight.

The menu would consist of both rolled cheese and beef enchiladas, tacos, nachos, refried beans, Spanish rice, flour tortillas, tostadas and salsa for dipping, and pecan pralines for dessert. She and Betty Kelly planned the party to be held in Betty's family room for all of the local relatives. Betty pledged to watch Mary prepare the meal, helping when she could, and offered the use of her kitchen.

Mary packed two cookie tins full of tostadas, and I located several cans of Old El Paso corn tortillas (which have since been discontinued by the manufacturer). We carefully wrapped several jars of mild picante sauce to prevent their breakage. We packed cans of refried beans, mild enchilada sauce, and two boxes of Spanish rice mix. Mary packaged *masa harina* for making flour tortillas into zip-lock bags. The pecan pralines were carefully wrapped in another cookie tin.

We later realized that the *masa harina* in clear ziplock bags greatly resembled bulk cocaine, and that could cause a stir should the suitcase carrying all the ingredients be searched at any of the three airports we would travel through. As it turned out, the bag made it through the baggage process without a problem. Whew!

That suitcase must have weighed a ton.

All the local relatives, plus three others, showed up for the feast. Mary wore a bright red Mexican peasant dress with all the colorful embroidery. My contribution to the Latin atmosphere was my asking Mary where she had hidden the Corona *cerveza*.

Betty and Mick's son, Fergus, and his wife, Eileen, arrived early to help set up the small family room with chairs, TV trays, and tables. P. J. and Esther and their daughter, Áine, and her fiancé, Kevin, and another daughter, Orla, and her husband, Maurice Ryan, arrived soon after. They were followed by Una and Seamus Hayes and Seamus's brother and two nephews who had just flown in from New York, along with Una and Seamus's son, Seamus Jr. Counting Mary and I, there were eighteen of us to be served—and Mary and Betty filled the plates and set out a basket of tostadas, bowls of salsa, and a stack of homemade flour tortillas.

I thought the kinfolk might be a little apprehensive about eating such spicy food. At that time, ethnic foods were nowhere to be found in Ireland, and the usual Irish diet did not include chili seasoning, jalapeño slices, or mashed pinto beans—salsa was unknown.

Apprehensive? No way. Our relatives dug into the Mexican smorgasbord like it was bacon and cabbage with a kick. Mary had made cheese enchiladas especially for Eileen who was a vegetarian. She let the others have their choice of beef or cheese enchiladas, or one of each. Of course there was no Corona, but there was plenty of Guinness and Harp lager, and I recall seeing several Budweiser cans when we cleaned up the kitchen later.

The pecan pralines were also a novelty for our Irish cousins. Filbert hazelnuts and walnuts are the most commonly available nuts in Ireland. The pralines were history in short order. No food was left—everyone was filled to the brim. They were ready to say adiós to the fiesta and adjourn the party to Eldon's at half nine.

Mick, celebrating his birthday and always light-hearted, acted as if the hot food was heating him up inside by wiping sweat from his brow and hurling it onto the kitchen floor. Seamus' brother Eamon, an employee of an American airline company stationed in New York, raved about Mary's cooking, claiming it was better than anything he could find in New York.

Of course, today there are so-called Mexican food restaurants in Ireland, and most of the ingredients we had to transport from Texas are readily available in the supermarkets. You can find some frozen Mexican dinners and, occasionally, some chili peppers on the produce tables.

It was a night to remember, and, even now, the Irish kin still talk about it. On succeeding trips, Mary only had to take some chili seasoning to make chili con carne for them. I don't know whatever happened to that red, embroidered Mexican peasant dress she wore.

*   *   *   *

MY COUSIN MARCELLINE seldom left the dairy farm on Puget Sound. When she was able to get away from the daily chores, she might be able to drive into nearby Tacoma or Seattle for shopping. But extended vacations were pretty much out of the question—flying to Ireland to meet her relatives was only a dream.

After Mary and I returned to Texas, we planned a short trip to visit Marcelline and her son, Ken. We scheduled some sightseeing along the Washington and Oregon coasts, but our main purpose was to show Marcelline the video of our recent trip to

Ireland. It contained many scenes of Clonmel and other parts of Ireland, a family get-together at P. J. and Esther's house that included all of the relatives living in Clonmel, and the Mayor's Reception that Kevin had recorded. Before we flew to the Northwest, I telephoned Marcelline and asked that she get a VCR and attach it to her television—she was very excited about finally seeing photos of the members of her family that had been mentioned in all the letters she had received from Agnes Powell and Betty Kelly over the past forty years.

Because of her failing health, we had planned for only two days with Marcelline and Ken. But during that short stay, our conversations were nonstop—we told her everything we had learned about the family, and she brought up all the tidbits she could remember from the transatlantic correspondence in the past.

Marcelline never stopped smiling; she asked that I play the tape over and over again. She especially dwelled on the late evening party at P. J. and Esther's home because Betty and Mick, Una and Seamus, Joan and Sean Howlett (in town from Galway), Áine and Kevin, P. J. and Esther, and Mary and I were all together in the living room of the family home at Old Bridge. Marcelline was tearful during each playing of the video.

After our visit, Mary kept her abreast of family news and we sent Marcelline photographs from our later trips. Her health continued to fail, and she died in 1994.

*   *   *   *

WHEN WE RETURNED in 1992 for our third holiday, we rented a self-catering apartment at Marlfield House, just a few miles west of Clonmel. Marlfield House is a three-story English manor house situated on several hundred acres on the north bank of the River Suir. Those hundreds of acres are covered with huge trees that must be hundreds of years old. The estate has riding paths, rolling hills, and two gate houses. Several acres along the frontage road have been converted to an athletic field used for soccer, Gaelic football, and hurling. Wild rhododendrons and other flowered plants and shrubs cover the rolling hills. The River Suir, only a few yards behind Marlfield House, was crystal clear as it tumbled down toward Clonmel. We could still see the old foot paths along the river's edge where horses pulled barges upstream many years before. The river was full of trout and salmon. The location was idyllic.

Marlfield House, west of Clonmel, dates back to the 1700s.

Marlfield dates back to the late 1700s, but it has been well kept by its current owner, Dennis English, who has remodeled it several times and reconfigured the rooms and hallways to accommodate both full-time tenants[1] and tourists. When we were guests there in 1992, it had about ten apartments, most of which were leased to long-term tenants, and a few were available for self-catering renters. The entrance to our Marlfield apartment was through the adjoining conservatory, a large hothouse with hundreds of different plants hanging from pipes and others stacked on rows of wooden tables. A misting system kept the plants watered but also kept the humidity up at a high level. Fresh flowers were cut daily and placed throughout the public areas of Marlfield House.

The apartment itself was furnished with antiques, heavy drapes, and flowery carpets. The only thing of recent vintage in the living room was the television. The kitchen was fully furnished—all we needed to bring was our food. The beds were soft—too soft—but we got used to them and the morning backaches.

The Marlfield pub was located in the basement, directly beneath our apartment. That was only a problem on the weekends when Mr. English brought in a local rock-n-roll band—the insulation was ineffective against the steady pounding of the bass instruments and the drums. We read a lot during the late hours on Friday and Saturday nights. Despite that glitch, however, Marlfield was an excellent accommodation. The living room was large enough that we could entertain our family instead of them having to entertain us. We had plenty of space in the dining area as well.

---

1. Construction of an 18-hole golf course, new homes, and remodeling of Marlfield House began in 2007. It is being renamed Marlbook.

I will never forget one particular early morning scene. There was a beautiful horse standing along the bank drinking from the River Suir, and the entire area was blanketed in a heavy fog. I took several photographs of that eerie scene, and it remains one of my all-time favorite views in a country famous for its vistas. Unfortunately, with heavy fog and it being too early for any sunlight, the photographs are too dark for reproduction.

*   *   *   *

OUR CLOSE FRIENDS living in the Horseshoe Bay community in the Lakes region of Central Texas knew about our frequent trips to Ireland, and they wanted to go there themselves. Who better than Mary and John to show them around when they could go? All they wanted was for us to tell them when we were going back—they would have us help them plan their trip to coincide with ours. That was okay with us because we wanted to show them just what a wonderful place Ireland is to visit. I pledged that they would love the lifestyle of the Irish people as well as the scenery and its famous "forty shades of green."

With the expectation of four different groups of our friends spending time as our guests, we had to find a special accommodation for the trip we were planning for the summer of 1994. This would be our fourth Irish holiday, and it would be after a two-year gap since our last trip.

We knew we would not want to stay at Marlfield again since we would need more space than just an apartment. We needed a minimum of three bedrooms and washer/dryer facilities for both our use and that of our guests. We needed a house.

St. Patrick gave a sermon at the Rock of Cashel in about 454 A.D. Tourists flock to these ruins in County Tipperary.

In searching for housing for the summer trip, we carefully read and studied the Irish Tourist Bureau's self-catering catalogue and finally narrowed our choice down to a four-bedroom home located in a rural setting near Ballymacarbry in the Nire Valley, five miles south of Clonmel in County Waterford. Its amenities looked great on paper, and the picture in the catalogue showed a beautiful home on a gorgeous hillside lot that was covered in flowers and trees with wild blackberries growing from large vines along the edge of the driveway and the road in front. It seemed to be just what we needed to accommodate both ourselves and our friends, who were, by then, chomping at the bit for their trip to begin. Some of them were already drinking Guinness to get in the mood for the good times ahead.

I telephoned P. J. in Clonmel to describe the home and discuss its location. He told me it was a beautiful area, "just over the mountain" from his house and that he "would drive out and have a look-see." He might, he said, be able to negotiate a lower price since we would be renting it for four weeks and, besides that, he had a lot of friends in the area. Within a few days, P. J. phoned back, gave the Nire Valley house two thumbs up, and told me he had made a reservation for us. The only thing the landlady needed was a deposit check and the exact dates we would be there. I sent her a check for the $200 deposit that same day, reserving the house for most of June—it was a done deal.

In order to work in a few rounds of golf, we stretched our trip from four to six weeks, adding one week at the beginning and another week after our rental period ended so that we could attend several rounds of the Irish Open golf tournament, staged by the European Professional Golf Association, scheduled to be played at Mount Juliet, a gorgeous one-time horse farm which had been converted into a top-of-the-line golf resort just outside Thomastown, some twenty-five miles east of Clonmel in County Kilkenny. All the best Irish, British, and continental European golf superstars were entered, along with a couple of the top American players. What a six-week trip we had planned for 1994!

*   *   *   *

AFTER WE GYPSIED around the West of Ireland for several days, traveling through Counties Clare, Kerry, and Cork, we arrived in Clonmel on Friday, May 31. P. J. and Esther invited us to spend the night with them since we could not check into the Nire Valley house until the following day.

Although it is usually awkward to spend a night in another's home, I was tickled pink by their invitation. My grandfather had been born in that house in 1881 and, although some alterations had been made in the downstairs area in the past, the second floor was untouched except for a periodic painting and, maybe, new wallpaper. From P. J.'s knowledge of the history of the home, he suggested we sleep in a front corner bedroom which he believed would have been the one that children such as Mary Ann would have been assigned while she and her husband, John Francis Walsh, were living with her parents. But that detail did not matter—just sleeping in the same house in which my grandfather had been born 113 years before was enough for me. I could not stop my mind from wandering back those many years, trying to put myself back in that time, living as my ancestors had, sharing their ups and downs. That was prior to John being sacked by Murphy's, so it was probably a happy time for them.

And it was a happy time for me. I don't believe I have ever spent as much time perusing any house as I did studying the older part of that home, the stairway to the bedroom floor, and that particular bedroom. The lawn and garden contained mature trees and shrubs, and I wondered how it looked back in 1881. I was certain the River Suir in front of the house was probably the same, although the park along the riverbank was probably new. I was equally certain much of downtown Clonmel and historic Irishtown, just west of downtown, was just like it was then. I knew for a fact that Sts. Peter and Paul Church in downtown Clonmel was exactly the same as it was when my grandfather was born, at least according to both the church clerk and P. J. That's the church where my great-grandpar-ents—John and Mary Ann—were married in 1875.

Not many of us are so lucky to have a chance to spend the night in the same house where at least four—maybe five—gen-erations of ancestors have lived and raised their families. And the current generation was welcoming family members from another country.

Time Capsule
1940 to 1950

America: The Japanese sneak attack on Pearl Harbor kills thousands and cripples the American naval fleet. Congress declares war and the economy switches to military footing. Armed forces swell with enlistees and draftees. Food rationing alleviates some shortages. President Roosevelt dies. Allied forces storm Europe. The German forces surrender. President Truman approves the use of atomic bombs against Japan in Hiroshima and Nagasaki. Japan surrenders. The Cold War with Russia begins.

Ireland: Eire maintains neutrality in World War II, but many men join British forces. After sixteen years, President de Valera and *Fianna Fail* are voted out of office. *Fine Gael*, the party of the free state, takes control and John Costello becomes Ireland's first prime minister. Ireland drops its free state status and declares itself a republic, affirming its 1937 claim of sovereignty over Northern Ireland. Britain guarantees its support of Ulster.

Family: The U.S. Cavalry assigns Mike Welsh to motorcycle duty, leading troop convoys across the country, but he develops tuberculosis and is first confined in military hospitals and finally discharged. Bob Welsh joins an Army railroad battalion, transporting equipment in North Africa and Italy. Bob joins John and Stene and his brother, Mike, in the family business when a second store is opened. Nellie becomes bedridden and is confined to a nursing home due to her suffering from Parkinson's disease.

Guests ... and Eldon's!

THE NEXT MORNING, P. J. led us to our holiday home in County Waterford. The landlady, Mrs. Greenslade, met us and showed us about the house, explaining the hot water heater (called a hot press), the heating oil, the washer and dryer, and the television. She pointed out that one room—a living room— was off limits because it contained some of her personal items that she did not want to move during the summer months when she rented out the house. It was locked up.

It was about that time that we encountered our first problem—the refrigerator did not cool and the broiler did not broil. It was the weekend, and the following Monday was a national holiday when most businesses would be closed. Fortunately, we worked around the problems. The broiler was repaired that same Saturday, and the refrigerator was rigged temporarily to provide some cooling and was finally replaced, though grudgingly, by Mrs. Greenslade the following Saturday in plenty of time for the arrival of our first guests.

We had mailed detailed maps to our guests so they would be able to find the house when their planned trip brought them to our countryside, hard-to-find, behind-the-wild-blackberries Nire Valley home.

*   *   *   *

OUR FIRST GUESTS were Dan and Dorothea O'Neill who were close friends and retirees living in Horseshoe Bay, a golf community in Central Texas' Lakes region. Dan was a golfing buddy of mine—he was still capable of shooting in the mid-seventies every round, even though he was in his sixties. Before settling into retirement, Dan had spent his entire working life with 3M Company, which made a lot of sense since both Dan and 3M were from Minnesota. He was a born salesman, and he had risen through the ranks to an international sales manager job in the Philippines, then into company headquarters as a top executive in Minneapolis. Dan was a large man: over six feet tall and 220 pounds, many of which he had added during his retirement and his after-golf relaxation in the Horseshoe Bay lounge.

He was jovial—seemingly always in good humor—and a friend to everyone he met. Dorothea was the silent boss of the family. She kept close track of their children, all of whom were married with their own families. She was very active in the Horseshoe Bay church. On Sundays, Dan put on a tie and accompanied Dorothea to church, but he was probably checking his golf calendar during the sermon. Somehow she kept Dan under control.

Besides golf, Dan loved Jack Daniel's Tennessee whiskey. His standing bar order was a "double Jack Daniel's and club soda," and every barman in Central Texas had best remember that if he hoped for a big tip when serving Dan. He loved to pick up the bar tabs—Dan was very generous in that regard—and he would not let you share the check. Dan usually got his way.

Dan and Dorothea O'Neill and author John Welsh (right).

About a month before we left for Ireland, we had Dan and Dorothea to our Texas home for an evening meal. This was my excuse to introduce Dan to Guinness—the Irish stout and the world's largest selling brew—which he said he had never tried. I carefully poured the Guinness Draft from the special black can, allowing the caramel-colored stout to settle to the top of the glass, turning black layer after layer, until it finally settled with a light tan-colored, creamy head about half-an-inch thick, ready to drink. Dan took a small sip—like he would if I had given him a glass of castor oil—and licked some of the Guinness head from his lips. He meditated for a few seconds and then proceeded to drink along with the rest of us. But I could tell: Guinness was not going to replace Dan's Jack Daniel's and club soda. Dorothea was a teetotaler and enjoyed her Diet Coke.

So Dan and Dorothea arrived in Ireland on schedule for their two-week trip. We helped settle them in for the three days they would spend with us. We set up one day for golf and two days of sightseeing in the immediate area around Clonmel. We had also worked in two nights in Eldon's pub with some of my relatives, especially Seamus Hayes who was a mean golfer himself and, like Dan, a jovial, good-natured, outgoing guy.

Dan, with his O'Neill surname, was of Irish blood and back home in Texas he was constantly reminded of his Irish heritage. He was proud of his Irish roots—I could easily sense his joy at finally being on Irish soil and mixing with the locals.

The night prior to the O'Neills arrival, I checked with Eldon at the pub to make certain that his bar stock included Jack Daniel's. Eldon dug around among the bottles at the back of the bar shelf and finally located a fifth of Jack Daniel's. He grabbed a damp bar towel and wiped the dust off the bottle, relieved to find one. I was quick to point out that my visiting Yank friend was strictly a Jack Daniel's man and would be in the pub tomorrow and the following night.

So at about 9:00 p.m. on the day the O'Neills came in, we made our way from the house to Eldon's where Seamus and Una had cornered a large booth. I explained to Dan how the Irish paired off and took turns picking up drinks from the bar, paying for the full round. It was out of the question for Dan to pay for more than his share of the drinks. He reluctantly agreed. I handled the first round and took Dan up to the service area at the bar so he would know where to go and what to do when his turn came up.

Eldon's sister, Máiréad—a golfing buddy of my wife Mary—was tending bar that night. I ordered the drinks for Seamus and Una, for Mary and me, and for Dan and Dorothea. I reminded Máiréad that Eldon had a bottle of Jack Daniel's set aside at the back of the bar shelf. She remembered, reached for the Jack Daniel's, unscrewed the cap to pour Dan's drink—and the bottle was empty!

Now, Jack Daniel's may be very popular in the United States, but it is way, way down the favorites list in Ireland. Most Irish drinkers stick with Guinness, but those who want whiskey prefer Jameson or Powers or Paddy's (Northern Irish prefer Bushmill). Máiréad apologized for the empty bottle, then raced from the bar into Eldon's adjoining liquor store to retrieve another bottle of Jack Daniel's. She returned shortly with a fresh one, but I could detect a little reluctance on her part to cut the black seal and open it up, remembering how long they had stocked the previous bottle. Before Máiréad opened it, she turned toward Dan and asked, "How long are you going to be here?" I intervened.

"Máiréad," I said, "Don't worry about it. Dan will be drinking Jack Daniel's tonight and tomorrow night. Open it up." She was relieved and prepared our drinks. Dan and I carried them to our booth.

As we settled down—the women on one side of the booth and we gents on the other—Seamus noticed that Dan had mixed his drink with the club soda, and opened up a conversation.

"Dan," he asked. "Have you tried the Guinness?"

"Yes, I have, Seamus," Dan answered. "John served me Guinness at his home before we left. I found that you have to develop a taste for Guinness."

"Ah, yes," replied Seamus. "I've been developing a taste for Guinness for forty-seven years!"

That short, funny conversation sealed a new friendship between Dan and Seamus. Dan sent Seamus a Christmas box for several years containing an assortment of 3M products, his way of expressing his friendship.

That conversation was probably the highlight of their trip to Ireland, especially Dan's. He repeated that entire conversation—word for word, Irish brogue and all—every chance he got when he could work it in at the Horseshoe Bay bar. I've heard it myself dozens of times, and I still laugh. I found out later that Eldon's had almost no Jack Daniel's left over after the O'Neills departed. That nearly empty bottle is probably still collecting dust at the back of Eldon's bar shelf.

*   *   *   *

THE O'NEILLS LEFT for Dublin on a Friday, and we had a few days to ourselves before the second batch of our friends from Horseshoe Bay was scheduled to arrive. Mary took advantage of this time to entertain many of our family living in Clonmel. They all wanted to see the house we were leasing, and this provided the best opportunity to do both without interrupting our evenings at Eldon's.

Betty and Mick, along with Fergus and Eileen, drove out on Saturday for a noon meal. While Betty and Eileen helped Mary in the kitchen, Mick and Fergus explored the grounds surrounding the house. Mick admired the flowers, shrubs, and trees, but he couldn't resist telling us how a few changes here and there would help the appearance of the property—he still loved working with the soil as he had for so many years. Fergus and I viewed the lawn in a different way—we both commented about the large amount of grass that would need mowing.

P. J. and Esther joined us after church the following day. Mary and I attended morning Mass at the Nire Valley Catholic Church which was located across a narrow road from a fast-moving stream that flowed out of the mountains between Ballymarcarbry and Clonmel. The noise from the water was clearly audible from our pew in the old church which dated back two hundred years. There were only a few parishioners at the morning Mass, and they were practically all up in years. It was clear that young people in the Nire Valley are like their contemporaries elsewhere—they don't attend church regularly.

P. J. and Esther arrived a little after noon. P. J. seemed a little disappointed that we weren't having Mary's Mexican food for Sunday dinner.

*　　　　*　　　　*　　　　*

IT WAS A busy time in the world of sports. The 1994 World Cup of Soccer was underway in the United States, and Ireland was one of the twenty-four national teams that had qualified. The United States Golf Open was also underway, but, in Ireland at least, the World Cup of Soccer was the big attraction.

Matches were played all across the U.S., and the time difference of four hours between coasts in America plus the five-hour
time difference between our East Coast and Ireland created
some viewing problems. But all the matches involving the Irish
team were played at times of the day that allowed live televising
to Ireland. The pubs were jam-packed hours before the matches
began. Everyone anxiously awaited Ireland's first match against
the heavily favored Italians, broadcasted direct from the New
York Giants' football stadium.

Eldon himself had constructed a tall stand, maybe eight feet
in the air, in the corner of his pub that elevated the TV screen
so that it could be seen from all corners of the bar. He draped
the stand in huge Irish flags, proudly displaying the tricolors of
the Irish team. The placement of the TV brought some
well-intentioned criticism from his patrons.

"Jeezuz," exclaimed one. "If ye put some candles on each side
of the telly, it will look just like the altar."

"No priest from Clonmel would ever hold Mass in this bar,"
shouted another. "The service is too poor."

"And, if he did, he wouldn't get a quid in the plate from the
whole bunch here," another retorted.

Eldon paid little attention. He knew every one of the jokers,
and he would continue to serve them despite their critique of
his festive stand. He had Máiréad and two of his regular bar-
tenders serving drinks (one of them was only "pulling" pints of
draft Guinness, the demand was so great). Eldon was bringing
plates of fried chicken, finger sandwiches, sausage rolls, and
other assorted snacks to each table and booth. Eldon's wife was
busy in her upstairs kitchen preparing food for the evening.

There are no time-outs in soccer; the action only breaks at
halftime. So, most patrons had at least two drinks in front of
them in preparation for the forty-five-minute first half. It would

be an enjoyable evening—especially if the Kelly green-clad "lads" could beat their swarthy opponents wearing the dark green and red uniforms. Mary and I shared a booth with Seamus and his young daughter, Mary Rose, who was home visiting from Dublin.

Most Americans are not thrilled watching soccer, mainly because the matches are usually low scoring or often even scoreless. But to soccer fans, that is the beauty of the game—tight man-on-man defense, cat-quick bursts with the ball up the sidelines by the upfront strikers or midfielders, heart-stopping saves for the goalies and leaping "headers" by everyone on the field. Even the "dives" by the Italians, when they were trying to draw fouls, were well acted but almost always ignored by the referee.

The veteran Ray Houghton gave the Irish fans the first thrill of the contest, when he scored in the eleventh minute of the game. The rest of the match was white-knuckle time. The mood of the fans in Eldon's alternated between very loud and silent, optimistic and pessimistic, elated and worried as the match wore on. But at the end of the ninety-minute match, the Irish had held on to win 1-0. As the final whistle sounded, Eldon's erupted. It was past 11:00 p.m. and there were still ninety more minutes of drinking-time before Eldon's closed. Forget the chicken, sausage rolls, and finger sandwiches—bring on the drinks!

*　　*　　*　　*

NO ONE EVER accused the Irish of being slow-on-the-draw. Even though the result of the match was not decided until after 11:00 p.m., enterprising Irishmen were hard at work. Early the next morning, white T-shirts were available across the country, brightly silk-screened in green ink with the message:

PIZZA CAKE!
IRELAND 1
ITALY 0
I still wear mine on special occasions.

*   *   *   *

ON THE FOLLOWING Wednesday, Barry and Marion Lynch from Horseshoe Bay arrived after driving through Southwest Ireland en route to Clonmel. We met them at Melody's, another one of our favorite pubs, which is located in nearby Ballymacarbry. After a welcoming drink, we returned to the house. Barry washed two loads of clothes while Mary and Marion prepared an evening meal.

Melody's Pub in Ballymacarbry, County Waterford.

But, just as quickly as we finished eating, we all returned to Melody's for the weekly session of Irish music performed by locals playing a concertina, piano, and guitar and taking turns singing. Melody's bar is divided into two areas: a game section with a pool table, and a lounge containing a few booths, a couple of tables, and a padded bench around the remainder of the walls. The piano is pushed up against the wall next to the booths. The lounge is designed to accommodate about twenty people, but there must have been thirty of us there for the music, which was great. You couldn't cut through the cigarette smoke with a chainsaw. Through the haze, we could pick out the concertina player, Nora, who we had heard sing in the Nire Valley Catholic Church the previous Sunday.

The next day, we escorted the Lynches to all the nearby sights: the Tipperary Crystal plant in Carrick-on-Suir, Langton's Restaurant and Bar (named Ireland's Bar of the Year on many occasions) in Kilkenny, the newly restored Kilkenny Castle, and the Mount Juliet Resort in Thomastown (the site of the upcoming Irish Open golf tournament). Then we stopped to buy renowned Wexford strawberries from a vendor on the side of the road as we headed back to the house—via Melody's.

*   *   *   *

SOCCER FANS TAKE the sport very seriously, especially true in those countries bordering the Mediterranean and in Central and South America where soccer is almost a religion. Colombia was the top seed in Group A of the 1994 World Cup, but lost its second match to the United States 2-1 when the Colombian goalkeeper, Andres Escobar, accidentally kicked the ball into his goal as the U.S. was threatening to score. Escobar had committed what is called an "own goal," and it is probably the worst thing that a goalie can do.

That certainly was the case for Escobar. After their upset loss to the Americans, the Colombian team returned home for a few days of rest, and shortly after their arrival, a vengeful fan murdered Escobar. It was the big news of the World Cup—television replays of the "own goal" episode seemed to be playing around the clock worldwide. Everybody recognized the name Escobar, even the Irish.

Ireland's second match was against Mexico. Eldon's was as packed as before, even though the match began at 5:30 p.m. in Ireland. Fergus and Eileen joined Barry and Marion Lynch, and Mary and I. We had arrived early enough to grab a booth. The bar was fully manned and Eldon's wife was busy in the kitchen again making sandwiches and heating sausages. Someone—it could have been Eldon himself—had placed a small votive candle beside the TV atop the flag-draped stand.

Mexico's Luis Garcia, however, took all the fun out of the evening, scoring two goals midway through the match. John Aldridge got Ireland on the scoreboard in the eighty-fourth minute, but it was too little and too late. In the final two minutes, the Irish goalie, Packy Bonner, narrowly avoided an own goal when he accidentally diverted a wayward Mexican attempt toward the Irish net.

Even though Packy's diversion missed the goal, it brought out some of the dark humor that Irishmen are famous for:

"Packy," bellowed a disconsolate patron, "does the name *Escobar* mean anything to you?" That comment turned around an otherwise dispirited group in Eldon's. It was Mexico 2, Ireland 1—heartbreak.

Barry and Marion Lynch left the following morning for Dublin to catch the fast ferry across the Irish Sea to Holyhead, Wales. They had planned another week of their holiday in England and Scotland, ending up in London for their flight back to Texas. We greatly enjoyed their company, and I'm certain they had a great time in Ireland.

*   *   *   *

THE TWO REMAINING groups of Texas friends arrived within hours of each other on the following Monday. Our close friends, Gene and Gerry Kirby and Gerry's brother, Bill Robinson and Bill's wife, Carol, arrived shortly after our niece, Angela, and her husband, Sam Bassett, drove in from the County Cork area. The following morning Sam, Gene, Gerry, and Mary played golf, and I took the others for a drive through the Clonmel area, all of us winding up at the Clonmel Golf Club for lunch.

The first round of the World Cup was winding up. The big match that night was between Ireland and Norway, a match Ireland could not afford to lose if the team was to move ahead into the second round, when all losers go home.

The eight of us arrived early at Eldon's and were joined by Fergus and Eileen. The match had an early 5:30 p.m. start time, so we were able to commandeer the largest booth in Eldon's. The crowd started to drift in, and sandwiches and warmed sausages were placed on every table and booth—the barkeeping staff was taking orders, ready for another big evening.

John and Mary Welsh enjoy World Cup
Soccer at Eldon's Pub in Clonmel.

It was a hard-fought match, but neither team could score. The 0-0 result meant Ireland moved on which made the crowd in Eldon's happy and insured a full house until closing time, and another full house when the second round began.

*   *   *   *

AT THAT TIME of the year, the sun sets very late in Ireland—after 11:00 p.m. The ten of us returned to the Nire house so that Gene and Fergus could take photographs of a gorgeous sunset from the steeply-inclined backyard which provided a spectacular view.

We spent the following day sightseeing at the Tipperary Crystal plant and Langton's restaurant in Kilkenny. Sam and Angela left that evening for the ferry to Wales at Dublin's port Dún Laoghaire, and the remaining foursome headed to Dublin the next morning. This wound up our entertaining of four groups of friends. It had been a lot of fun but also a lot of work for Mary. All the activities at Eldon's pub had been a big help in providing entertainment while our guests were in County Tipperary.

We ended our vacation the next weekend. After checking out of the Nire Valley home, we stayed a couple of nights in Margaret Whelan's bed and breakfast. We spent those last few days among the gallery at the Irish Open golf tournament at Mount Juliet and watched the second round of the World Cup. It was the saddest night of all in Eldon's as the Irish team lost to Holland 2-0 in the knockout round.

We packed up the next day and drove east to Naas in County Kildare to visit P. J. and Esther's daughter, Fiona, her husband, Sean, and their two children. Then we drove through the Irish midlands to Westport, Galway, and then on to Shannon for the flight back to Texas. It had been an outstanding six weeks. Now, more than ever, we envied the Irish lifestyle and wanted to be a part of it, if we could work it out somehow.

That was our next project.

Time Capsule
1950 to 1960

America: Communist North Korean troops storm across the Thirty-eighth Parallel into South Korea, and, under auspices of United Nations, President Truman orders American troops into battle. Chinese Communist forces intervene. Armistice is signed three years later after thirty-five thousand Americans die. The Supreme Court ends school segregation. Rosa Parks sparks bus boycott in Alabama, and Martin Luther King rises to lead the civil rights movement.

Ireland: Religious conflict heats up in Ulster. Unionist Protestants have complete control of Northern Ireland Parliament, and give Catholics no part in government. Catholics feel treated like second-class citizens and a sense of disquiet surfaces. Russia vetoes Eire's application to become a member of the U.N. because of its neutrality in World War II, but Ireland is admitted in 1955. IRA begins campaign against the British and the Unionists in the North.

Family: Nellie Welsh dies in 1954 after a long illness and is buried in the family plot in Hannibal. The Welsh brothers open El Paso's first supermarket in 1952 on Fort Bliss military reservation and replace the original store with a second supermarket two blocks away. Dozens of children are born in the Jones, Powell, Welsh, and King families in Ireland and the U.S. The two sons of John and Stene join the Welsh family business. Plans are drawn for a third supermarket.

CHAPTER SEVEN

Considering a Relocation

AS THE YEARS passed, we spent more and more time in Ireland. Mary and I felt more comfortable there and more a part of our Irish family and the lifestyle they led. We were no longer there as tourists, and we made friends outside the family. We were familiar with all the churches in Clonmel, the golf courses in Clonmel and nearby Cahir, the employees in the Superquinn supermarket downtown, and some of the owners of the pubs we frequented. We recognized the television news announcers, and we loved watching both Irish and English sporting events. We had become accustomed to picking up the hometown weekly *Nationalist* newspaper when it appeared on the newsstands every Thursday morning. A lot of our activities had become a daily ritual, even a habit. It was almost like home.

When we first traveled there in 1988, we had noticed a big difference between the Irish and Americans. The Irish were much more relaxed, easy-going, and less intense. They lived each day to the fullest. They found time to visit with their neighbors, to stop and chat if they ran unto a friend on the street. They were aware of—but not consumed by—world events and the news of the day. They left politics to the politicians and laughed at them when they were too full of themselves.

The Irish were beginning to accept the inevitability of joining the new European Union. Full participation meant that they would have to accept a single currency and open their borders, but they would also enjoy the freedom to travel across old national boundaries and carry a single passport.

The English are opposed to the single currency idea—they believe the pound sterling is the monetary yardstick of the world. And the growing strength of the French and Germans in Europe is hard for the English to accept.

The European Union began pouring money into Ireland—its resources were funding new superhighways, remodeling old castles, improving port facilities, and generally trying to bring the Irish infrastructure up to speed. Air flights between Dublin and Shannon to all points of Europe were more plentiful and reservations were getting harder to obtain. German, French, and Dutch travel buses were everywhere in Ireland during the summer months and were especially noticeable at landmarks such as the Cliffs of Moher or the Rock of Cashel or the Ring of Kerry. The slower pace of golfing at Ballybunion and Lahinch had stepped up to a point requiring weekday tee times, caddies were scarce, and the green fees and other costs were rising.

Yes, the advancing European economy was infiltrating Ireland but the Irish were still slow to accept it, even though the European projects had been a shot in the arm to their economy. It seemed as if all these changes were a lot more significant in Dublin than they were in the outlying counties—our family simply shrugged them off. Ireland may have been becoming more European, but the Irish people were still Irish. We hoped it would stay that way.

Mary Welsh and Orla and Maurice Ryan at Cliffs of Moher.

*   *   *   *

IT WAS IN about 1993, after the trip when we stayed at Marlfield House, that Mary and I first talked about spending more time in Ireland, maybe even moving our residence from the Texas hill country to across the Atlantic.

To even consider relocating, we had to do a lot of thinking about our circumstances. We were retired, primarily spending our time on golf courses at Horseshoe Bay and, occasionally, traveling to Far West Texas where we still owned several small-town Welsh's Supermarkets. Other than the normal nags of old age, our health was satisfactory. My diabetes was controlled by medication, so that was no immediate problem.

Our youngest son, Joseph, was the general manager of our grocery business and was doing an outstanding job, requiring very little of our time to help with the supermarkets. He was putting his own stamp on the business, and we felt that his dedication to its improvement gave us the opportunity to enjoy our retirement. Some of the profits from the business, along with our social security checks, provided us with an adequate income, and our residence was free of a mortgage and our cars were paid in full. All of these factors gave us an independence that we had never before discussed.

So spending more and more time—even moving—to Ireland wasn't beyond our grasp. We started talking about it more often and more seriously.

We decided that our first step should be to find out all we could about those matters that tourists never consider: the price of housing, the cost of an automobile, the availability of health insurance (since we could possibly lose our Medicare), our liability to Ireland for income taxes from our American business, the expense of moving furniture and household goods overseas, our eligibility for any Irish social benefits since we both held Irish citizenship, and any other taxes we might face. We agreed that we would share the tasks of obtaining this information from the appropriate offices in Ireland. Mary would organize it all into notebook form.

This welcome sign takes advantage of the popular
World War I soldiers' song "It's A Long Way to Tipperary."

Much of the information we needed was available in various Irish newspapers and publications, and we were able to summarize that quickly. We wrote to offices in Dublin seeking pamphlets and brochures, subscribed to *The Nationalist* newspaper for the classified ads, and made contact with a real estate firm in Clonmel. A quarterly publication, *Inside Ireland*, was very informative for anyone considering retiring there. But the most critical data we needed came from VHI (the national health insurance service). It might be very important to us, depending upon the length of stay we decided upon.

We continued to gather information and took advantage of our trip in 1994 to complete our notebook and obtain answers to questions.

When we returned to Horseshoe Bay in July 1994, we became more serious. We contacted moving companies to obtain precise costs of shipping furniture and other household and personal goods should we decide to relocate permanently. We also needed to know the costs of long-term storage of these items should we decide to sell our home and relocate for an undetermined length of time, just not permanently. We had a lot of balls in the air and decisions to be made.

*   *   *   *

TO MOVE PERMANENTLY was a major decision. We had our children to consider, even though they either had families of their own or were adequately stable in their lives. We had the absence from our grandchildren to consider. We had our friends and close relatives to consider, and even though those relationships would not change, we would still be a long way from them and would see them infrequently. We had the inevitability of declining health because of age to consider, even though we would be insured in Ireland and would still be able to fly back to the States for any needed treatment as long as we kept our Medicare current. And we had our business to consider. Even though it was being managed well, our distance from it could become a problem.

Some of our children thought a long-term visit would be a good idea, but they thought that considering a permanent relocation was crazy. The other children's responses were noncommittal.

We could only discuss the issue for so long—the time finally came to make up our minds.

Our decision? Why not split the two alternatives? We thought we'd take simple steps, one at a time, without carving anything in stone. Just let things unfold.

First, we decided to fly to Ireland for several weeks to find an apartment or home to rent or lease, purchase an automobile and the electrical appliances we would need, get enrolled in the VHI health plan, explore any tax consequences, line up the utilities for our accommodation, and take a good amount of clothing with us on the upcoming trip, the rest of clothing to follow when we returned for a longer period of time. After accomplishing these tasks, we would return to Horseshoe Bay to make arrangements for the furniture and our home, wind up our affairs, and notify all those concerned about our new residence for whatever length of time it might be.

We immediately telephoned Fergus Kelly to help us search for an automobile. He was somewhat of a car buff, and he had a good relationship with several dealers in Clonmel. He willingly took on the task of checking out the prices, conditions, and availabilities. With the extremely high Irish tariffs on automobiles, buying a new car was out of the question for us, so we asked Fergus to concentrate on late model used cars with basic extras and options. Manual transmissions were okay since all the rental cars we had used in previous trips had been stick shifts. "Go to work, Fergus, we'll be there in about two weeks." We also called the real estate agent we had talked to previously, and he agreed to check through his listings for available apartments, single-family homes, or duplexes.

We lined up our round-trip flight reservations and packed the large amount of clothing we had planned to take with us to leave there. We were very excited. Our longtime dream of living with the Irish was about to come true!

OUR FIRST STEP after checking into Mrs. Whelan's bed and breakfast, was to touch base with all of our family in Clonmel. We had been keeping them up to date as we had weighed our decision about moving, so it was no big surprise to them when we knocked on their doors. They were anxious to help in any way we needed.

Fergus was Johnny-on-the-spot. He had prepared a list of available cars at several different car dealers and had created his own rating system. He and I looked at all of them, about eight or so, and I finally bought a four-year-old Nissan that had belonged to a widow who had recently died. It was in tip-top condition and had less than forty thousand miles on the odometer. It had the basics—manual transmission, radio and tape deck, and a four-cylinder engine that got more than thirty miles per gallon of petrol. The paint and upholstery were in excellent shape. Including Ireland's value-added tax (VAT), we paid the Nissan dealer £7,500 Irish, the equivalent of $12,000 based on the exchange rate at that time. I realized I could have bought a similar car brand-new in Texas for the same price. Oh well!

Our realtor, Pat Quirke, had grown up in Clonmel and was heavily involved in his family's real estate business. He had been helpful to us in our previous conversation over the long-distance telephone lines. By the time we arrived, he had prepared a relatively short list of homes and apartments that were readily available. He took us to two different houses, but they were both several miles out of town and did not suit our needs. Then he showed us a small apartment along the quay downtown, across the street from the River Suir. It was only two blocks from P. J. and Esther's home in Old Bridge, where my grandfather had been born in 1881.

***Mary Welsh on the front stoop of our apartment
on the River Suir in Clonmel, County Tipperary.***

The apartment was small—and I mean small. Downstairs, there was an entry hall with a small table for the telephone and the stairwell to the upper floor. Off the entry hall, there was a parlor with a love seat, an arm chair, an end table, and space for a television beneath two large windows overlooking the river and the street in front. A tiny dining area was off the parlor, furnished with a white pine table with two benches. Next to the dining space was a mini kitchen containing about four feet of countertop, a typical European refrigerator (it was about four feet tall), a four-burner electric range oven, and a few cabinets above the sink and counter. A combination clothes washer/dryer was next to the sink. The freezer compartment of the refrigerator provided room for two ice trays and about two small packages of frozen food. It was a one-person kitchen, no bigger.

Upstairs, there was a master bedroom with a double bed and a wardrobe. There was also a full bathroom and a small bedroom with a single bed and a small wardrobe. In the hallway, a large closet was filled with a hot press, which Americans would call a water heater. The hot press was electric and expensive to operate. And it heated water slowly. We only ran the washer/dryer at night because the electric rates were substantially cheaper between 10:00 p.m. and 5:00 a.m. We turned on the hot press about fifteen minutes before running the shower in order to get enough hot water and then shut it off promptly after bathing.

The bottom floor was carpeted, and the upstairs had beautiful hardwood flooring. But that was it—there was no back door, no garage, no front porch. There was a small stoop with three steps up to the front door. A planter box for flowers next to the stoop also served as a storage compartment for the wheeled trash bin, appropriately called a wheely-bin. The apartment was within a complex of about ten units, most of them were about the same size. A Dublin lady had bought ours two years before as an investment, but she had never seen it, much less lived in it. Yes, it was small, but we felt it would suit our purpose well as we contemplated what our final decision about a permanent move would be. We agreed to a six-month lease at £350 Irish, or about $600 U.S. a month.

One of the best things about the apartment was its location. Not only was it close to downtown and to P. J. and Esther's home, but it was within three blocks of three Catholic churches, in easy walking distance to the Superquinn supermarket, the movie theater, and about ten pubs. There was a newsstand one block away on the main downtown street and several nice restaurants were located near our apartment.

Though not a city by American standards, Clonmel is a large town of about eighteen thousand, and the central downtown district has every type of business and shop you could ever need. The post office and library were also convenient.

We were making progress getting settled. We had our car and an apartment. We bought bedding and linens so that we could move from the bed and breakfast, had Fergus accompany us to an appliance store that he had recommended, and purchased a television and an electric teakettle—a must-have in Ireland. After getting all the utilities turned on and signing up for the television cable service, only two items remained on our must-do list. We needed to talk to an accountant about any income tax problems we might encounter and sign up for the VHI health insurance.

Brian Mordaunt, the Nissan car dealer, was very helpful when he found out from Fergus that we were contemplating moving to Ireland. When I told him I had questions about any Irish income tax I might owe from my American business, he quickly set up an appointment with his chartered accountant for that afternoon.

His CPA studied my U.S. tax return for 1995, made several pages of notes, and finally estimated that I would owe about an additional 7 to 8 percent of taxable income to Ireland. This was after credits and charges from the two countries' tax tables. That was not good news. The amount would not be staggering, but it was certainly more than we had expected. And that percentage could go higher if our business income from the supermarkets increased.

It was the first negative note we had encountered.

The nearest VHI office was located in Limerick, about fifty miles north of Clonmel. We drove there the following day. We located the office in the heart of the busy downtown and waited our turn for an interview.

The young lady registrar called us both into her cubicle. Mary signed up first. She provided all the answers to the usual enrollment questions, and after the registrar referred to premium tables on her computer, we were informed that Mary would owe about £275 Irish ($400 U.S.) for the full year. This covered all hospital services and charges, surgeries, and doctor visits, and required only a £10 co-payment to the doctor.

Top row: downtown Clonmel, the historic Main Guard
Bottom: River Suir quay, weir at Old Bridge, and Gladstone Street.

The services VHI provided were not as complete as the typical American insurance plan. Under VHI, you could only seek services from a specialist after approval and recommendation by the general practitioner, there was a waiting list for most elective surgeries, and the hospitals themselves were not exactly state-of-the-art. But the price was right—a little over $30 a month in U.S. dollars! We wrote out the check, and Mary was covered by VHI.

Then it was my turn. The registrar began entering my name, address, date of birth—and then—Rejection! Her computer stopped proceedings as soon as she entered December 18, 1929.

"That makes you more than sixty-five years of age," she said.

"That's right," I replied. "I turned sixty-six last December."

She apologized. "I'm sorry, sir. You can be a member of VHI with full coverage until the day you die no matter how old you may be, but you cannot register for membership after the age of sixty-five."

"Are there any appeals?" I asked. "I have read all the pamphlets and brochures I received from VHI, and nowhere did I read of the exclusion past sixty-five. I was under the impression that VHI was open to all Irish citizens, regardless of age. Had I known about this requirement, I could have signed up last year, just to be registered when we moved here from the States."

"I truly am sorry, sir," she answered. "I wish I could give you some hope for a different decision, but I can't. You can appeal to the Southeastern Health Board, or the VHI offices in Dublin, but I must advise you there will not likely be an exception to our rules and regulations.

"One thing I can do," she continued. "I can enroll you for a limited hospital coverage for £10 Irish per month, but there are many exceptions to admission under that policy. It is better than nothing though."

Both Mary and I were shocked. Nowhere had we seen this rule, and that included all the other publications we had read as well as all the literature from VHI.

"Thank you for your trouble," I told the registrar. "We are disappointed, but you have been most kind. We will keep the coverage for Mary and will think about the hospital plan you offered me."

She responded, "Remember, you can cancel Mrs. Welsh's policy at any time, and it will be pro-rated and any credit will be reimbursed. There will be adjustments made for any services she has used, but your policy is worth keeping at this time."

We left. We headed for a pub that we had noticed only a few doors away. We had encountered a second negative note—it was a big loud one.

*　　*　　*　　*

AFTER A FEW long sips of Guinness, I finally spoke up.

"Look," I said. "We have leased an apartment for six months. We have bought a car for about twelve grand. We have bought a TV and a teakettle, and we have come this long way to live with the Irish.

"Let's do this. When our return flight comes up, let's return to Horseshoe Bay. We'll take our house off the market and make arrangements with our buddy Pete (our lawn maintenance contractor) to watch things while we're gone. Then we'll buy another round-trip ticket to Shannon (airport) with an open return date, and we'll spend at least the next six months here and do what we planned to do in the first place. We'll live out our apartment lease.

"Moving here permanently is now out of the question, but so what? We can have one hell of a vacation in Ireland for six months. What do you think?"

"Sounds great to me," Mary replied. "This may be best anyway. Let's do it!"

The new plan erased the disappointment we had felt only moments before. After a few days, I felt confident that we could sell the car before we left, but if we couldn't, we would find a place to store it for our next trip to Ireland. It was sort of like the old saying: "If you have too many lemons, make lemonade."

Time Capsule
1960 to 1970

America: John F. Kennedy is narrowly elected president in 1960. He is assassinated three years later. Other political assassinations follow with the deaths of Robert Kennedy and Martin Luther King Jr. Civil rights unrest picks up speed in the South, and President Lyndon Johnson introduces sweeping laws against racial discrimination. Congress agrees. Astronaut Neil Armstrong is the first man to walk on the moon. Anti-Vietnam War protesters march on Washington.

Ireland: Organizations demanding equal rights for Catholics are formed in Northern Ireland, beginning thirty years of violence, including political unrest, fighting in the streets, and bomb attacks in Ireland and England. The IRA and Sinn Fein are in the midst of the turmoil. British troops arrive to restore order. Paramilitary forces are formed in Unionist areas to combat the IRA. A march of Catholics is ambushed at Burntollet Bridge in Derry, and three hundred are injured.

Family: Following a short career as a merchant marine seaman, P. J. Powell becomes a mainstay in Clonmel, operating a pub and becoming active in *Fine Gael*—the conservative political party. His brothers-in-law are employed in county governments and in a farming operation at national hospitals. Military cancels the lease on the Welsh's first big store located on Fort Bliss property, but two new Welsh supermarkets are opened in El Paso.

CHAPTER EIGHT

Living Among the Irish

TWO WEEKS AFTER our disappointment at the VHI offices in June 1996, we flew back to Texas. We invited our close friends over for drinks to tell them about our trip and the decision we had made after the VHI episode. Needless to say, they were happy that we would only be gone for a short time, and they all volunteered to watch our house and take care of any problems while we were away.

I made arrangements with Pete Illing, our yard guy, who would continue to take care of our lawn, check the pipes and water heater inside the house regularly, pick up our mail twice a week and send it Global Priority to our apartment in Ireland with two-day delivery. This would enable us to keep current with our monthly bills, and we had someone who would take care of our residence. We had worked with Pete for about seven years, trusted him thoroughly, and were confident that he would take care of things properly and promptly.

We pulled the house off the real estate market and advised the household movers of our change in plans.

We were able to get flight reservations to depart again within a few days. We wrapped up the final details, said good-bye to

141

everyone again, and boarded a Delta flight in San Antonio bound for Atlanta and Shannon.

After landing in Shannon, we were met at the airport by our cousin, Orla Ryan, P. J. and Esther's daughter, who lived in Limerick with her husband, Maurice. When we had left Ireland two weeks before, we had parked our car at their home so that it would be available when we returned. We dropped Orla off at the Shannon Ulster Bank branch she managed, and drove the sixty-five miles to Clonmel and our humble abode across the street from the River Suir.

It was now about July 1, and the Irish summer was upon us. The daily temperature was a more-than-comfortable sixty to sixty-five degrees Fahrenheit. It was weather for shorts, polo shirts, and sandals or sneakers. Summer is a short season for Ireland, but the Irish take full advantage of it. We could smell charcoal fires in the residential neighborhoods, foam coolers and barbecue grills were out for sale in the stores, the outdoor patios at the pubs were in full swing. Few places had air-conditioning, but it was not necessary anyway. Those days of sixty to sixty-five degrees turn into forty- to fifty-degree nights, and a sweater or light jacket felt comfortable.

Our Irish relatives—the ones we had grown so fond of since we had met almost seven years ago—were glad to see us back. They seemed genuinely disappointed with the outcome at the VHI office, but they approved of our decision and welcomed us into their homes and into their family circle. We were full-blown members of the family, and we were included in every occasion or get-together that took place from our return until we flew out some seven months later.

It was like this—our name was Welsh, their names were Kelly and Powell and Hayes and Howlett and Hazard, but we were all just branches of the same tree named Jones—going all the way back to Mary Ann, Patsy, and Joanna Jones and their parents Thomas Francis and Mary Casey Jones. And the center point was the white stucco two-story house in Old Bridge across from the River Suir in Clonmel—the house occupied by P. J. and Esther. I never heard if anyone had figured this out, but I wondered just how many children had been raised within that house during the past almost two hundred years. I know for sure that at least one has been nearby for more than 125 years— Margaret Mary Walsh, the second child of John Francis and Mary Ann Walsh, died of tuberculosis as a child and is buried near the side of Old Bridge House in a small cemetery that once adjoined St. Nicholas Catholic Church. It had fallen into disrepair, had been abandoned, and had finally become a vine-covered ruin.

Betty Kelly and John Welsh outside the gate of the cemetery at ruins of St. Nicholas Church at Old Bridge.

I don't know if it was Alderman John Kennedy and his Clonmel Cemetery Restoration Committee or Seamus' County workmen, but somebody had mowed the grass in the cemetery, carefully trimming around the headstones. I took the time to straighten a few of the markers when I searched for Margaret Mary's gravesite.

*   *   *   *

MY WIFE, MARY, has never known a stranger. She is outgoing and has a great smile. She is happy to make new friends and enjoys new adventures. I would not call her an extrovert, but she mixes well with others. Her two passions are singing and golfing, and she does both very well.

With at least six more months to enjoy Ireland with our family and friends, Mary dove right in. She tackled golf first.

We had played the course at the Clonmel Golf Club on many occasions during our previous trips. It was well kept by golfing standards, the fairways were heavily grassed and mowed regularly, the greens were of normal size and smooth for putting, and the sand traps—though limited—were strategically located and served their purpose as a hazard. The course meandered over and around and up and down the very hilly terrain south of Clonmel in County Waterford. It had a small pro shop and a very nice clubhouse with offices, locker rooms, and a restaurant. A fine bar overlooked the course.

Those hills were a problem for Mary and me. At that time, only a handful of Irish golf courses had electric or gasoline carts available for its players, and those had only a few. Clonmel had none. The club president and golf captain (they ran the club during their elected terms) decided that walking was an integral part of golf, and they would not break tradition by bringing in golf carts. Besides that, the gasoline carts were too noisy, and the electric ones didn't have the power to go up and down hills for very long.

So, we discovered the Cahir Golf Club, located about fifteen miles from Clonmel. Cahir was not level by any measure, but its hills were gentle and the course was in good condition. For old-sters like us, the flatter terrain was much easier on the knees. Cahir had no carts other than the ones you push or pull, but that was fine with us because the walking was excellent exercise, and the scenery around the course was spectacular. Seamus had a membership at Cahir as well as Clonmel, so he introduced us to the office staff, and we joined the Cahir club at a cost of £100 Irish for an entire year, about $160 U.S.

It took only a few rounds for Mary to decide to join the ladies' association. They played every Tuesday morning, rain or shine. Occasionally, I accompanied her to the course and used that time to practice my own game while she played with her new buddies. She continued playing with the ladies' association for the next few months before the winter set in, and she made several close friends through the association's weekly outings.

But singing occupied a lot of Mary's time. She had opportunities to sing weekly and to travel to Wales with the outstanding choir of St. Mary's Church to compete against other choirs from both Ireland and Great Britain. She sang her way into a solo part in a local playhouse musical review that was televised nationwide across Ireland. She was sought out to sing at a large wedding of a prominent Clonmel couple. The main benefit, however, was the numerous friends she made through the choir, the musical review, and the subsequent parties and get-togethers. Though no singer myself, I became a part of the fun events because spouses were included—for financing purposes, I concluded.

*   *   *   *

ST. MARY'S WAS not the largest of the four Catholic churches in Clonmel. It was located on the west edge of the downtown area in a section known as Irishtown, which dated back to when the ruling English gentry confined the native Irish to shanties and smaller homes outside the wall that surrounded the town. The original St. Mary's parish dates back into the early 1500s. The church itself was located within the town walls, but years later the church was taken from the Catholics and given to the Anglican Church of Ireland. In due time, the Catholics built a new church in Irishtown and, since it was a part of their heritage, used St. Mary's name for its newly established parish. Irishtown is separated from the downtown district by a multi-storied, castle-like structure with gun turrets on top and a narrow street below. The structure is called Westgate and is a historic icon of Clonmel.

The newer St. Mary's in Irishtown dates back to the 1850s. It was totally refurbished in the mid-1990s and serves the Catholic population of West Clonmel, along with the southern section across the River Suir in County Waterford. St. Mary's main chapel is only a few hundred yards from the river's bank.

There is no pronounced rivalry between the various Catholic churches in Clonmel. Sts. Peter and Paul's, situated in the middle of the downtown area, is the largest building and its records date back for two centuries. Its sanctuary is very large and ornate and the chapel contains a small secondary altar off to one side. I became very emotional when I attended Mass there for the first time, knowing that my great-grandparents were married there in 1875 and my grandfather was baptized at the very fount that is still located on the large altar area at the front of the church.

The Bunratty Folk Park depicts a rural Ireland village in 1800s.

The hot water radiators recently installed down the center of the church do very little to warm the huge main chapel; I can only imagine how cold and damp that church must have been when my grandfather's family attended Mass in the mid-1800s. I suppose that was part of their penance.

Since it was the nearest church to the western suburbs of Clonmel, St. Mary's attracted many young people. This was reflected in what I observed to be the main difference between St. Mary's and Sts. Peter and Paul's—the older residents of Clonmel lived in homes near the downtown area while younger families lived in newer areas further from the business district and closer to St. Mary's.

Even though P. J. and Esther's Old Bridge home was actually closer to St. Mary's, they had always attended Sts. Peter and Paul like his parents and their parents before them. And, technically, Old Bridge was located within the boundaries of the Sts. Peter and Paul parish. They were the only members of the Irish family who claimed Sts. Peter and Paul's as their church.

Una and Seamus Hayes and Betty and Mick Kelly were regulars at St. Mary's. Mick was by far the most religious one of the entire family—he attended Mass every day without fail, often at the large Franciscan Friary in downtown Clonmel. St. Mary's was a little closer to our apartment than Sts. Peter & Paul's.

*   *   *   *

MY FIRST MEMORY of St. Mary's is from one of our early trips to Clonmel. Betty, Mary, and I were sitting near the aisle in the center section at the 10:00 a.m. Sunday Mass. As the collection plate was being passed, I could hear the parishioners dropping their coins into the wooden plate as it made its way down each pew. The £1 Irish coin at that time (before the introduction of the euro) was a little larger than the old American silver dollar coin, and it made a distinct noise when it was dropped into the plate. Mostly I heard the quieter sounds of the less-than-a-pound coins—the five-, ten-, and fifty-pence pieces. There were no church envelopes which are commonly used in America.

When the plate arrived on our pew—as was my weekly habit—I placed a £20 Irish bill into the plate, and passed it on to my right. There were about ten parishioners sitting on the remainder of the pew and, as the plate passed in front of them, each bent forward and looked to their left to see just who had put the £20 note into the plate.

We ate our Sunday midday meal at 2:00 p.m. that day at the Emerald Gardens, a Chinese restaurant downtown, with Mick and Betty, Seamus and Una, and P. J. and Esther. When there was a lull in the conversation, Betty loudly whispered to Una, "John dropped a *twenty* into the plate at Mass. It was the only bill in the plate." Everyone heard her.

"Jeezuz, John," P. J. exclaimed. "That's very generous."

I was a little embarrassed. "Well, that's my usual donation back home," I apologized. "It seemed appropriate to me."

*   *   *   *

THREE SEPARATE WINGS split off from the altar area of St. Mary's. Most of the parishioners, as a matter of habit, sit as close as possible to the same aisle and pew, week after week. Betty's habitual pew is in the center wing. The choir and organ are located on an elevated loft at the rear of the center wing.

The acoustics in the old building are magnificent. The priests used a wireless microphone, but it was probably not needed. The music from the choir and organ seemed to surround me, no matter where I sat. It was the outstanding sounds emanating from the choir that attracted Mary. It only took a few weeks for her to contact the choir director and audition. She was quickly accepted and began attending choir practice every Thursday evening in the parish hall across the street from the main building. At that time, there were about fifty voices in the choir and most of them had been members for years.

The Thursday choir practice was broken into two sessions. The singing session lasted from 8:00 to 10:00 p.m., and then virtually the entire choir adjourned to Carey's Bar, just down the street for the wrap-up session. It was Dutch treat—everyone bought his own drink. The choir members crowded around one end of the bar and seized as many booths as they could nearby. The owners, Michael Carey and his son Michael Jr., knew when the choir would be showing up and made sure that there was enough room. The regulars who made Carey's their nightly haunt made sure that they had a seat near the opposite side of the bar or they adjourned to a separate lounge area when the choir flocked in on Thursday.

The pub session lasted about an hour each week, and then everyone went home. Carey's was not a so-called musical pub— there was no singing or concertinas or guitars being played. It seemed as if the choir had enough singing during the rehearsal session—the time at the pub was for talking to friends over a Guinness or a cider or an orange drink.

Just as Eldon's was my Irish family's pub, Carey's was the choir's pub. Even though there were at least six other large pubs within two blocks of the church, no one ever considered going anywhere but Carey's. I even heard one male member of the choir jokingly remark that he wished Carey's had an organ in the bar so they wouldn't have to spend those earlier two hours—the rehearsal session—in the cold, unheated parish hall.

$$*   *   *   *$$

THE ST. MARY'S Choral Society, not affiliated with the church choir but containing some of the same members, performed in the White Memorial Theatre, just up the street from the Westgate. The theatre was opened in 1975 and had been named for James A. White, the founding musical director.

The structure was built in 1843 by William Tinsley at a cost of £600 Irish as a Wesleyan Methodist chapel, but it fell into disrepair and was eventually boarded up and abandoned. In the early-1970s, members of the choral society realized that the old building could be readily converted into a theatre with a balcony, a large stage and an adequate backstage area. Donations were gathered and members, doing much of the labor themselves, refurbished the inside and built themselves a place for their shows.

The society had a practice of putting on one show a year, usually the score from a successful Broadway performance. Friends and families of the choral members built props, sewed costumes, sold tickets, and ushered—all the support functions of a successful theatre group.

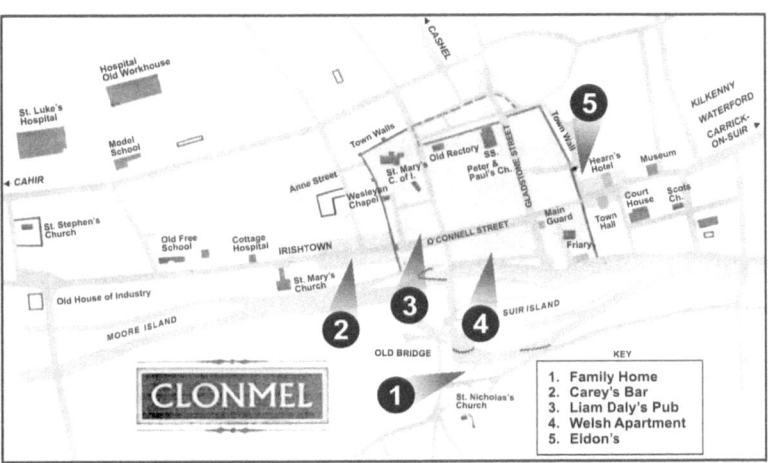

Map shows the downtown area of Clonmel, stretching along the River Suir.

Through her friends in the choir, Mary heard that the choral society would be holding tryouts for a big performance celebrating the society's twenty-one years of operation. The show would be named *Music of the White*, and would contain memorable songs and acts from all of the society's previous performances. Her tryout was successful, and practices were scheduled for every Tuesday night. It turned out to be another two-session practice, the first was always held at the theatre and the second at Liam Daly's pub near the Westgate, just down the street from the theatre.

Mary had parts as a principal singer in several of the skits, ranging from songs from *Showboat* to songs from *HMS Pinafore*. Of course, *Grease* was not in her league, being dominated by teenaged and twenty-year-old members of the society.

One skit was the White Theatre's version of the recent world-renowned performance by the Three Tenors—that the group appropriately named the "Three Sopranos." Mary and two other ladies—both prominent singers in Clonmel who had been in many of the society's previous presentations—comprised the trio. They were great. Maybe it was because they sang songs that reminded many in the audience of their younger days, but the sopranos drew rounds of applause and were one of the highlights of the entire show. Reviews in *The Nationalist* newspaper raved about the trio—Mary, Biddy Magnier, and Bernie Lonergan.

Music of the White was scheduled for five performances. One performance was televised live all across Ireland by RTE, the national radio and television network. Just the thought of being on national TV certainly brought out the butterflies for the members of the cast, but it also gave them an extreme sense of pride. They were all at their best when the cameras rolled.

As their many practices continued, Mary became well acquainted with members of the cast. As was her habit, Mary left our apartment one evening with only her door key because it was a hassle to keep track of her purse during practice. After the cast had finished its rehearsal, Mary was walking toward the apartment with several other female members who invited her into Liam Daly's pub for a drink.

"Sorry, but I didn't bring my purse," Mary answered.

"No problem. We'll buy the drinks."

That would not be the only time Irish generosity baled Mary out when she was without cash.

Time Capsule
1970 to 1985

America: Former President Johnson dies at the age of sixty-four. The Supreme Court throws out all state laws prohibiting abortions during the first trimester of a pregnancy. President Nixon resigns to ward off possible impeachment. Vice President Gerald Ford is sworn in. Americans evacuate Vietnam and the Viet Cong move into Saigon. A Three Mile Island plant leaks radioactive gas. Iran frees U.S. hostages. Ronald Reagan is sworn in as the thirty-ninth president.

Ireland: The IRA splits, and the Provisionals emerge. The British begin the process of internment without trial by jailing 342 Catholic troublemakers after an upsurge of violence. Three days of riots follow—twenty-two die and seven thousand flee their homes due to sectarian arson. Derry protest march ends as British troops kill thirteen on Bloody Sunday. The British suspend Stormont government and govern directly from London. Over 2700 die in Ulster over a twenty-year period.

Family: John Welsh dies in 1974, and the last supermarket is sold. Stene Welsh's cancer worsens, and she dies in 1975. Their two sons are employed in food wholesaling, but John Jr. and his wife, Mary, purchase a supermarket in Alpine, Texas, in 1983. P. J. Powell suffers severe hip problems in Clonmel and becomes active in an Irish organization for handicapped persons. Some Powell family members are employed by U.S. pharmaceutical and software firms in Ireland.

CHAPTER NINE

A Regular Routine

ONE EVENING A young lady knocked on our apartment door and told me that she wanted to talk to "Mary, the lady who sang at the White musical." I escorted her into our parlor. It turned out she was a local physical therapist, Cathy Cashin. She was engaged to Bobby Nugent, the son of a prominent Clonmel real estate company owner. She said she had heard Mary sing at the *Music of the White* performance and wanted Mary to sing at their upcoming wedding.

Mary had sung for many weddings (and funerals) while we were in Horseshoe Bay. She and the musical director of a Horseshoe Bay church were a team—Karen Carson played the organ and piano and Mary sang. They were usually paid $150 each to perform several songs during a ceremony.

So, when Miss Cashin asked Mary how much she charged, she could only respond by saying she made $150 in Texas, which would equate to about £100 Irish. Mary said she would sing as many songs as requested and the young lady wrote out the check right then. She gave Mary the name and telephone number of the organ accompanist who resided in Limerick and suggested that the two of them get together before the ceremony to practice.

The wedding was to take place in Holy Trinity Abbey, a famous old church in the village of Adare in County Limerick about fifty miles northwest of Clonmel. After we arrived for the Saturday afternoon wedding, Mary and I explored the church.

The Norman Trinitarian Order built the original structure in the year 1230—yes, 1230! A tower was added in the 1400s, and other changes and restorations were made in the intervening years. It has been a monastery, a hospital, and a convent at different times. Today, it is in fine condition, and it is difficult to believe that its history dates back 775 years.

After the organist arrived and he and Mary began rehearsing, I walked to all corners of the sanctuary to check out the acoustics. They were perfect—you could hear a pin drop. There was no echo at all.

A priest from Dublin, who was a relative of the groom, conducted the ceremony. As is a custom in Irish weddings, just before the ceremony ended, the priest led the bride and groom and the other wedding attendants to the sacristy at the back of the altar to sign the registry and appropriate records. The guests waited patiently in their seats, and Mary sang "On Eagles' Wings." And she sang and sang and sang. And the organist played and played and played—verse after verse after verse.

After an extended period of time, the priest returned to the altar and apologized for the lengthy delay. He advised the guests that a required portion of the vows had been accidentally overlooked and that he had to perform that missing portion before the ceremony could end. The missing portion had to do with "worldly goods," so after the priest read the required words, and after both parties agreed to it, the ceremony ended.

Holy Trinity Abbey in Adare village dates back to 1230 A.D.

Thatched-roof shops in Adare village, County Limerick.

The aisles of the church were blocked and everyone had to exit down the center aisle. After the wedding party marched down from the altar, the bride and groom remained at the back of the church at the end of the center aisle to personally greet each guest and thank them for attending. This portion of the ceremony was filmed and was a nice keepsake and remembrance of their wedding.

A well attended reception was held at a hotel in Adare, and many of the guests partied on until the wee hours and stayed at the hotel for the night. We returned to Clonmel, having spent an interesting day inside a centuries-old church at a wedding in which Mary sang dozens of verses of the same song and the priest forgot to include part of the vows.

*   *   *   *

THE ST. MARY'S church choir was invited to participate in the 1996 International Choir Competition Festival in Llandudno, Wales—a quaint resort town on the Irish Sea, near Wales' border with England. The event was scheduled for November, an off-season time when the hotels would be available to house the forty-odd choirs that would be competing.

The details were worked out. The choir, a few spouses, and one of the church's priests, Father David, would board a large bus on Friday, ride to Dublin's port at Dún Laoghaire, and travel on the huge hydrofoil Stena Lines ferry to Holyhead in Wales. The ninety-mile trip across the Irish Sea took only ninety minutes.

The ferry had several levels for vehicles only, including levels for buses, semi-trucks and trailers, motor homes, hundreds of automobiles from European countries, motorbikes, and rack after rack of bicycles. Passengers lounged on a gigantic enclosed deck, which also housed a McDonalds, two other fast-food restaurants, a casino, a day care center, and a duty-free shop. Comfortable booths and lounge chairs filled the big room.

After docking in Wales, we reboarded the bus for the ninety-minute ride from Holyhead to Llandudno and checked into the four-story residential Belmont Hotel that the choir had reserved. Guest rooms were located on the three top floors, and the reception area, a bar, and a restaurant filled the ground level. The hotel sat across the street from a sandy beach and a promenade along the western edge of the business district. You could hear the waves clearly as they splashed ashore. It was November, and the Irish Sea was gray and topped off with huge whitecaps as it crashed over the beach.

On that Friday night, the choir transferred from the restaurant bar to a large pub across a side street. And, unlike the usual Thursday nights at Carey's, this time the choir sang—and sang their hearts out. They were truly enjoying the preparation for Sunday's competition.

On Saturday, the entire group took the bus to Chester on the English side of the Welsh border. It was primarily a sightseeing trip—Chester is the size of city that American tourists would appreciate more than, say, overcrowded London or Paris or Barcelona. Streets in the Chester business district are lined with two- and three-story commercial buildings. Sidewalks are located in front of the shops on both the ground and second floor. It looked like apartments occupied the top floor on the taller structures. Shoppers packed the sidewalks, the restaurants, and the bars. Even though it was almost winter and the weather was chilly and damp, several sidewalk cafes were open and their patios were being used by hearty souls. It was old European architecture at its best. I loved Chester and its old churches and buildings.

The competition was an annual event for Llandudno. Male choirs, female choirs and mixed choirs competed against each other, and one overall champion was judged as best. Each choir marched out onto the stage and stepped onto triple risers. Each had its own piano accompanist and its own director. Each sang two songs of its choosing, although the second had to be a different kind of song than the first. Each wore its own performance uniform—the women of St. Mary's were dressed in long black skirts and white blouses, and the men wore tuxedoes, white shirts, and black bow ties.

St. Mary's was the only church choir. The others were civic choirs or school choirs from colleges and universities, and all of them were excellent. St. Mary's did well, placing above the median in the mixed choirs group. No one felt disappointment—each member knew that he had performed up to his ability, singing against the best choirs in Wales, Scotland, England, and Ireland.

The choir had just as much fun riding the bus back to Clonmel on Sunday evening as it had had going to Wales on Friday. As one of those interested spouses who had been willing to pay £75 Irish for travel, a ticket to the competition, and some meals, I had a great time—one I won't forget.

*   *   *   *

IT MAY SEEM that Mary's singing and our golfing left us little time for our Irish family, but that would not be true. Several times a week, we walked from our apartment along the River Suir across the stone Old Bridge to visit P. J. and Esther. On the days when the weather permitted, we sat on the patio that overlooked the front lawn and flower garden. The garden was lovely, thanks to Esther's hard work.

P. J. was considering hip replacement surgery because his hip joint was in bad shape. Doctors blamed its degeneration on his use of too much cortisone in earlier years. He needed a cane to get around, but he did so very well even though he weighed about 250 pounds—or almost eighteen stones as they measure weight in Ireland (one stone is equal to fourteen pounds). P. J. could still drive, but he preferred to spend his time at home reading, watching television, talking politics, or preparing for an evening at Eldon's.

Una Hayes had been having lung problems for a long time, and during recent years, she had needed a constant supply of oxygen to help her breathe. Her weakened condition forced her to spend much of her time in bed, and she had spent some days in a Dublin hospital. She was unable to leave the house very often, but we visited with her frequently.

Seamus was nearing retirement. He played golf as often as he could, but he was very busy managing the affairs of the southern portion of County Tipperary. Still, he would seldom miss his nightly card game and his pints of Guinness at Eldon's, both starting promptly at half nine.

Betty Kelly and Mary became extremely close. Betty was happy every time we drove to their home to visit or to go shopping downtown. Betty was a typical homemaker, concentrating on duties in the kitchen, doing the laundry, and other household chores. Mick took care of the lawn and the outside of their home and ran most of the errands since Betty did not drive. He read two newspapers every morning and occasionally watched television, especially if there was a sporting event on the schedule.

Betty and Mick had three daughters, Carmel and Suzanne (who were twins) and Elizabeth. Carmel, a nurse, and her husband, Fritz, had lived in Baghdad for some time. Fritz was there on assignment for Siemens, a German company. Suzanne and her husband, Martin, and their three children had recently returned to Ireland after living in South Africa, where Martin had worked as an architect. The eldest daughter, Elizabeth, her husband, Eamonn, and their three children lived outside of Naas in County Kildare. Fergus, his wife, Eileen, and their child, Mikey, lived in Clonmel where Fergus was an environmental officer with Merck, Sharpe, and Dohme, the large pharmaceutical company that operated a sprawling plant just outside of Clonmel.

I enjoyed keeping company with Mick. Even though he was retired, Mick followed the same daily personal routine he had followed his entire adult life. He got up early, read the newspapers, attended Mass, and—now that he wasn't working in the fields and dealing with the animals—he now dressed like a gentleman farmer. His clothes were always spotless and freshly starched, his shoes were always shined, he was always clean-shaven, his hair was always neatly cut and trimmed. He remained extremely fit for a retiree. He washed and waxed his automobile whether it needed it or not. His garage was clean and orderly, his lawn neatly trimmed, and his plants and shrubs flourished. He was a creature of habit.

His closest friend had managed one of the hospitals, and the two of them met at a pub every Thursday at 8:00 p.m. This arrangement had gone on for years and years; Mick looked forward to "his night out" and would not have missed it for any reason. But then, about two years before we had leased our apartment, his friend died and the Thursday pub routine ended. Mick missed his friend, and he missed the fellowship they had—just telling stories and enjoying each other's company over a couple of drinks.

Michael Kelly managed the farm operation at two Irish hospitals.

Soon after we arrived in Ireland in late June, Betty told me that, after Mick's friend's death, Mick sat around the house each Thursday evening, acting crestfallen. I decided to try to do something about this situation.

"Mick," I said one day, "I can't talk much about farming and hospital work, but I can tell stories, and I listen well, and you know I enjoy the pub. So, how about this: I will meet you at any pub you choose at eight each Thursday while Mary is at choir practice, and we will have a few drinks together. How does that sound?"

"That sounds like something we would both like," he responded. "Only, I won't let you buy the drinks. Is that fair?"

"No," I replied. "We take turns. You buy, I buy, you buy, I buy. That's fair."

"Fine. I'll meet you at Eldon's at eight on Thursday. See you then."

That started a weekly routine which lasted more than six months, right up until the time Mary and I boarded the plane back to the States. It was a routine I cherish, and I have often wished we did things like that here in the States.

We rotated our Thursday evening session between Eldon's, Moran's, and Allen's, but we always ended up at Carey's where Mary and her choir gathered after their weekly practice.

I'm pretty much a creature of habit myself, so I followed a fairly rigid schedule on Thursday evening. I watched the evening news or some other program on television until about 7:40, then walked to whichever pub Mick and I had scheduled for that week. But no matter what time I arrived at the pub, Mick would already be there and have my drink waiting for me at our booth or table. So I started leaving home at 7:30, then 7:25, then 7:20, but it made no difference—Mick was waiting. I could not be the first one there. And he would not touch his drink until I sat down.

I loved that ritual, and I believe Mick enjoyed it too. Mick now resides in an assisted living home as the result of an accidental fall. He suffered some debilitation and can only get to a pub when escorted by a relative or a close friend.

I think about Mick's and my routine often.

AMERICAN RETAIL STORES used to start the Christmas season right after Thanksgiving, but that is now a thing of the distant past. They have moved the Christmas season up to the middle of October, and it is a sales plan that someone must have picked up from Irish merchants.

Ireland does not celebrate Thanksgiving—instead the country observes what they call Harvest. It is a time for ecumenical church services. The few Clonmel Protestant churches join with the slightly larger Anglican Church of Ireland congregation and, together with members of four Roman Catholic churches, meet in the old St. Mary's Church in downtown Clonmel.

The priests and pastors each give short sermons, all asking for understanding between faiths, and thank their God for the proverbial bountiful harvest of crops grown in the area. A joint choir sings hymns familiar to all the worshipers.

Since old St. Mary's had been converted from a Catholic church to an Anglican church in the 1850s, the choir sat in pews facing one another behind the pulpit and altar. Following her usual practice at choir rehearsals, Mary did not take her purse to the service to avoid the hassle with her purse. So, when a collection was announced, Mary was ill prepared. She had no money … again.

Embarrassed, she turned to a choir buddy sitting next to her.

"I didn't know they were going to pass a plate," she whispered.

"Not to worry," her friend replied, handing her a large coin.

Then from each side of her and from down each end of the pew came coins from other choir members. Mary was suddenly inundated with money. Blushing, she quietly dropped the coins into the plate, and tried to explain and thank everyone on her row. She could hardly wait for the next hymn to be sung.

This minor episode briefly embarrassed Mary, but, at the same time, she was impressed with the generosity of the Irish people. And she never left the apartment again without money.

*   *   *   *

WITH THE SHORT interruption for Harvest, the Irish Christmas season lasts from November 1 until the end of the first week in January. Our daughter, Jacque, was living in Seattle at the time, and she wanted to travel to Ireland again to celebrate Christmas with us before we returned to Texas in January.

Her three-week vacation was properly timed for her to share the Irish Christmas party season and the choir's Christmas caroling shortly before Christmas Day.

All the Clonmel hotels that have a restaurant, a pub, and a large dining room stage their own Christmas parties. They invite any and all residents willing to spend the equivalent of $25 to pay for a Christmas dinner, dancing along to the music of a local band, and a table shared with their friends. All of the hotels have an open cash bar for the parties. This is a fairly inexpensive way for Clonmel companies to treat their employees and spouses to a Christmas party without having to do it themselves.

The hotels begin their advertising for reservations soon after November rolls around. This was something new to us so we made inquiries to our relatives and they agreed that this would be something we could take back to Texas with us as a memory of part of the Irish Christmas season.

I made reservations for Jacque, Mary, and me at the Clonmel Arms Hotel, which was rated Clonmel's best along with Hotel Minella. Since it was located just off the quay two blocks from our apartment, we could walk there and not need to be out among partying drivers or subject to roadblocks put up by the local *garda* (police) on the lookout for drunk drivers.

We put on our best party clothes and walked to the hotel for our 8:00 p.m. reservation. It was a fun party. The music was loud, the young people were in top spirits, and the food was well prepared, served as a buffet, and included everything you could possibly want at a Christmas dinner.

The music was not our style, so we skipped the dancing, but the bar was well stocked with all our favorites, and that made the party complete. We lasted until about 10:00 p.m. and then walked back to the apartment for bedtime.

*   *   *   *

THE WEATHER IN Ireland in December is not good. The nighttime low temperature reading might occasionally dip below the freezing mark, but with the dampness brought on by the almost daily rain showers, the proximity of the River Suir, and a constant wind blowing all the way in from the Atlantic Ocean and the Celtic Sea, it was nasty. I thought I had been cold at other times—wrong. I had never been so cold, especially not so cold as when Jacque and I accompanied Mary and the church choir for their traditional Christmas caroling. I still shiver thinking about it.

The choir began their caroling at a nursing home, singing from the street out front. The patients loved it and some even sang along with the choir. But the main stops for the choir were the major Clonmel pubs, particularly the ten or so near St. Mary's Church in Irishtown and a few just past Westgate in downtown Clonmel. The pub owners had been alerted to an approximate time when the choir would make its appearance. This happened every year and the pub owners and customers looked forward to it, just like the choir did.

The fifty-odd choir members streamed into each pub and sang several Christmas carols. They only stayed long enough after that to pass a large can for donations. I don't know if the choir was *that* good or whether the customers and pub owner had had more than enough to drink, but the donations were substantial in each pub that the choir visited.

Even so, the carolers were not in-and-out in a hurry in every pub, no sir. After about every three pubs, the choir director called a short time-out, and the choir members took time for one drink before heading to their next stop. And even though the pub service was fairly quick, it was still a thirty-minute delay at least three times during the night. Experience had told the choir to begin the caroling no later than 7:00 p.m. so they could make the ten pubs on their schedule.

Jacque and I lasted for about an hour after the singing began. We were frozen. Liam Daly's pub was close by and it was one of the final stops of the night for the choir. It seemed like that was where we needed to be—out of the spine-chilling cold and into a toasty pub where we could enjoy the seasonal *craic* of Liam Daly's customers and a drink from the bar.

*   *   *   *

WE HAD THREE favorite pubs in Clonmel: Eldon's, Carey's, and Liam Daly's. Liam Daly's was the one located nearest our apartment, and it played a regular part of Mary's and my Sunday routine, which we followed, well, religiously.

The routine began at about half eight. After a big breakfast, I dressed for Sunday Mass at one of the three Catholic churches that were within walking distance—Sts. Peter and Paul's, St. Mary's, or the Franciscan Friary. To accommodate all parishioners, the three churches scheduled their Masses in rotation every thirty minutes—as an example, Mass would be scheduled at 8:00 a.m. at Sts. Peter and Paul's, at 8:30 at St. Mary's, at 9:00 a.m. at the Friary, then repeating at 9:30 a.m. at Sts. Peter and Paul, at 10:00 a.m. at St. Mary's, and at 10:30 at the Friary, and so on. That made it very convenient for a churchgoer like me who was not attached to a favorite church or priest—I could attend Mass when I wanted.

The routine continued after Mass, regardless of which one I attended. I walked from the church to the downtown newsstand where I bought the *Sunday Independent* newspaper, and returned to the apartment to read it. Meanwhile, Mary prepared for her noon Mass with the choir at St. Mary's and left the apartment at about 11:30 a.m.

By Irish law, pubs cannot open on Sunday before 12:30 p.m., without exception. At about 12:10 p.m., I walked the two blocks to Liam Daly's and stood outside with the same three guys every week, impatiently waiting for Liam to open his doors. At about 12:20, one of the guys would holler at Liam in his apartment above the pub, demanding that he open the doors. In his own sweet time, but always a few minutes before 12:30, Liam would open a side door to admit us while he turned on the lights and put his cash into the register. His timing was perfect—he knew what we drank, and he would begin pulling our pints of Guinness at precisely 12:30 p.m.

Clonmel patrons enjoy the Christmas season at Liam Daly's.

St. Mary's noon Mass ended at 12:30 p.m., and Mary walked the two blocks to Liam's pub. I had her drink ready and moved from the bar to a booth when she arrived. We stayed there until the bar closed at 2:00 p.m. and then either walked across the street to the Emerald Gardens Chinese restaurant for dinner or headed back to our apartment on the quay. Liam soon regarded us as regular customers, learned our names, and remembered them every time we visited his pub.

It is easy to understand why Liam Daly's was high on our list of favorites.

*   *   *   *

MARY'S FINAL PERFORMANCE with the St. Mary's choir came during the last week before our flight back to Texas in early January 1997. Undoubtedly, this performance was one that no member of the choir will ever forget.

Facilities at one of the national hospitals in Clonmel house non-violent mental patients. They receive necessary care and various treatments within the hospital. And one of their perks was an annual performance by the St. Mary's choir in their large activities hall.

About thirty-five choir members attended and put on one of their best shows of the Christmas season. They sang from risers furnished by the hospital. Forty-plus patients were seated around the walls and in front of the choir. They were almost raucous in their applause.

Hospital personnel had set up a long table full of finger foods and drinks of all kinds, including wine, beer, and whiskey. Everything was available for the choir *and* the patients. A local man had been brought in to act as a disc jockey for dancing after the choir performed. He soon had music blasting through the large speakers that he had set up.

As soon as the music started, some of the patients grabbed choir members to dance with, other patients were dancing with one another, and choir members were dancing with other choir members. Even the hospital attendants joined the party. It lasted for about an hour, and then the patients were escorted back to their rooms.

The choir partied on for a while and, knowing that this was the last time they would see Mary for quite a while, said their tearful good-byes. Finally, Mary started walking out, crossing the floor of the large activities room.

Another P. J.—this one P. J. Kelly who had been one of the main performers at the Choral Society's *Music of the White* show earlier in the year—gave Mary her final farewell.

"Mary," he said. "When you are back in the States, and when you think about this choir, just remember where we were in our last performance." The choir roared with laughter, realizing that they were performing in a mental institution.

It was a final note to a wonderful singing season for Mary—and P. J. Kelly's comment is still high among her memories of the seven months we spent living among the Irish.

*   *   *   *

AS I HAD hoped, the Nissan dealer bought back our car. We made a full recovery, except for the nonrefundable value-added tax we had paid up-front. The appliance dealer bought back the television set at a fair price, and we gave the other electrical appliances and items we could not ship back or pack to Betty.

It took a couple of days to do so, but Mary and I finally finished packing for our flight back to Texas. I had come down with a bad cold; I had a fever and felt terrible. But we said our good-byes to all our kinfolk. Seamus drove us with our luggage the sixty-five miles to Shannon.

We had an early morning flight, so we spent the night at the Great Southern Hotel near the Shannon airport. After checking in, I immediately went to bed, but we soon received a phone call from our cousin, Orla Ryan, the young lady who managed the nearby Ulster branch bank. She wanted to meet us in the hotel bar to say good-bye. I managed to get dressed, and we went to the bar for a couple of good-bye drinks. Mary stayed on with Orla for one final round after I returned to the room.

Early the next morning, we had a hotel porter load our suitcases and drive us to the departure area of the Shannon airport. We checked the luggage, converted our remaining Irish money into American currency and coins, and soon thereafter boarded the Delta plane bound for Atlanta and the first leg of another journey from Tipperary to Texas.

Outside, it was what the Irish call a dull day: it was beginning to rain.

Time Capsule
1985 to 2005

America: The space shuttle Discovery explodes after takeoff, killing seven astronauts. A fire destroys the Soviet nuclear plant at Chernobyl. President Bush orders attacks on Baghdad after Iraqis seize Kuwait, and Allied ground troops standby. President Gorbachev resigns, marking the end of the Soviet Empire. Voters reject Bush for reelection and elect Arkansas Governor Bill Clinton as the new president. U.S. House impeaches President Clinton, but Senate acquits him.

Ireland: The IRA declares a ceasefire, and loyalists follow two months later. All-party talks continue on and off. The IRA ends the ceasefire. The talks begin again. The IRA resumes the ceasefire. The Belfast Agreement is finally signed on Good Friday in 1998. After high unemployment in the 1980s, Ireland's economy booms in the 1990s. Ireland and ten other countries tie their currencies together with the euro—another step in the effort to unify Europe. Property values soar. Many emigrants return.

Family: Sean O'Keeffe, an officer in the Irish Army, serves several tours of peacekeeping duties for the United Nations in the Middle East and Israel. The Jones, Powell, Welsh, and King families continue to grow in Ireland and the U.S. Betty Powell Kelly dies in 1999. Joan Powell Howlett dies in 2002, and her husband, Sean, dies soon after. P. J. Powell dies in 2004, and Una Powell Hayes dies in 2005. Survivors hope to maintain newfound family ties.

CHAPTER TEN

It's in the Blood

FRIENDS HAVE ASKED us why we continue to travel to Ireland. "Why," they ask, "don't you visit Spain or France or Germany, even the Greek islands or Turkey? Get a different perspective of the world, broaden your horizons, see different sites, try different foods and drinks, spice up your lives."

Occasionally we travel with our youngest son, Joseph, and his wife, Liliana, and their children to Nuevo Vallarta on Mexico's Pacific coast where they have a time-share at the area's best resort. And, yes, we do enjoy the beach, the resort's amenities, and the golf courses—but mainly we enjoy the company of our son and his family. The weather is usually okay—it can be hot as Hades; it can rain when you least expect it; and it can be very windy. But, overall, the weather is satisfactory—we enjoy the trip every time we are asked to accompany them.

So why then do we keep going back to Ireland? Two reasons: one, we love to spend time with our relatives, although several have recently passed away; and two, we all speak the same language, and we can understand one another.

Well, almost. Ireland claims to have forty shades of green, and that is probably correct. But Ireland also has many different brogues, and although the words may be the same, they can be difficult to understand at times. And it is not only the brogues that are different—certain words can have totally different meanings from the ones that Americans understand.

I never really thought too much about that when we were there, but Mary did. She even made some notes. And a few years ago, those notes came in handy when she read in *Inside Ireland,* a quarterly periodical we received, that they would welcome comments from Americans who have visited Ireland.

Without telling me about it, she sat down with a pencil and a pad, composing a poem to express her feelings. *Inside Ireland* immediately published it, and because of comments she received from our family and friends, she submitted the poem to a book publisher who was going to print a collection called the *Best Poems and Poets of the 20th Century.* That title was probably a little overstated, but the publisher liked her poem and included it within his hardcover, tabletop edition. Here's the poem:

Life in Ireland

I haven't a clue why the weather is *fresh,*
Or a day is *dull* and a cabinet, a *press.*

I cook on a *hob* while I *hoover* the floor,
And I go for *messages* when I go to the store.

I put *petrol* in the car instead of gasoline,
And I keep a towel in the *boot* to clean the
      windscreen.

I drive on the left and steer from the right,
Minding *loose chippings* by day and *narrow margins*
      by night.

I park my car *tidy* and, to enjoy a scene,
I stop at a *lay-by* to see forty shades of green.

If the rain is *lashing,* I put up my *brolley,*
And, at the supermarket, I push a *trolley.*

If a child is *roaring,* he gets a *biscuit* for a *sweet.*
A *tart* is not what you think, but something to eat.

A fry is a *chip*, and a chip is a *crisp;*
I *post* a letter and give someone *a lift.*

I wear a *jumper* for warmth and *tights* on my legs;
I eat *bacon and cabbage* and *rashers and eggs.*

When asked, "How are you?" Or what kind of day
      you had,
The answer is usually: *thank God, not too bad.*

*   *   *   *

MORE THAN TEN years have passed since Mary and I spent those seven months living among the Irish and enjoying their lifestyle. Many events have occurred within the family—primarily the deaths of four of the five siblings of Agnes and George Powell.

Betty Powell Kelly's health was breaking down at the time of our extended stay, and she died in 1999. Joan Howlett passed away in Galway in 2002, and her husband, Sean, died a few years later. P. J. Powell died unexpectedly in his sleep in 2004, and in 2005, Una Hayes succumbed to lung problems that she had endured for many years. Mary Frances Hazard, the youngest daughter, is still enjoying good health in London. Both Mick Kelly and Seamus Hayes have recently been hospitalized for extended periods of time. The steady drumbeat of old age has taken a toll on my contemporary Irish cousins.

These deaths and prolonged illnesses have been very upsetting to Mary and me. Though she was very close to Joan, Esther, Una, and Mary Frances, Mary took Betty's death especially hard. Over the eleven years of their friendship, they had become as close as sisters—maybe closer. From those first letters in 1987 and 1988—and from that first evening meal when we met in Clonmel a few months later—Mary and Betty were the ones that really led the way in reuniting the Irish and American families after four generations.

Most of the children of the Powell siblings are busy in their careers and raising their children in various locations across Ireland. We hear from most of them from time to time, but only P. J. and Esther Powell's daughter, Fiona, and Betty and Mick Kelly's son, Fergus, keep in touch regularly. Fiona has her hands full raising two children and sometimes has to relocate overseas temporarily when her husband, Sean, is assigned peacekeeper duty as a commandant in the Irish army.

Both Fiona and Fergus are computer literate, but sending e-mail from Ireland to America is not virtually free of cost as it is here. Like using their telephone, the meter starts spinning when they log on to their Internet connection.

WE TOOK OUR next holiday to Ireland in September 2000. We leased a self-catering bungalow in the mountains north of Cahir, about twenty miles from Clonmel. The owners, William and Bridget Bourke, owned a dairy farm and two small bungalows which they rented to tourists. In order to get to the rental units, a tenant had to open two huge gates, cross a railroad track, close both gates, drive past the dairy farm's milking barns, and maneuver up a narrow unpaved road along a swiftly flowing mountain stream. The bungalows sit on the southeast side of the Galtee Mountains, and the scenery is gorgeous with wild rhododendron bushes and wild flowers and blackberries growing everywhere.

We arrived just in time for the traditional Anniversary Mass remembering Betty's death one year ago. Most of her relatives were there, and we all left the service at the Presentation Convent and adjourned to Carey's pub nearby. Meeting in the pub gave us a chance to talk to those we had not seen for a long time, but this visit was not the happiest of occasions.

The four weeks that we stayed in Ireland that time passed very quickly—we did some visiting, but we also spent a lot of time traveling to our favorite vistas along the south Irish coast near Annestown. Although Betty was the only one to have died at that time, it was just not the same as previous trips. Mick had spent a lot of time improving her gravesite, and we visited the cemetery with him while we were there. We miss Betty.

*   *   *   *

WE PLANNED ANOTHER trip for 2004, and we would be tour guides again. This time we would be escorting our son, Joseph, his wife, Liliana, and their two oldest children, Tori and

Johnathan, around the country. I made reservations for us at the renowned Hotel Aherlow outside Tipperary town, about twenty-five miles north of Clonmel. I reserved a three-bedroom lodge with a large living and dining area, a big kitchen, two bathrooms, and a large deck overlooking the scenic valley below stretching all the way south to Clonmel.

Except for a week in Munich when he was a teenager, this was Joseph's first trip overseas. He and his family had spent many vacation days at their time-share in Mexico, but this was Liliana's and the two children's first time to cross the Atlantic.

The teenagers had only a casual interest in Ireland. Their "I'd-rather-sleep-late" attitude about sightseeing slowed our daily tours to a crawl, but we were still able to take them to many of the landmarks we wanted them to see. We were able to take in the usual nearby points of interest. The six of us all made the trip to Cobh and the emigration museum, a place I deeply felt that they needed to experience.

About six weeks before we were all scheduled to be in Ireland, I telephoned P. J. and suggested that he organize a party at one of pubs for the family, especially those in their thirties and forties, so they could meet Joseph, Liliana, and the kids. P. J. and I had discussed this several times before. We both felt that it was important that the next generation of our families become acquainted and perhaps develop the same relationship that we had developed. He agreed that such a party as I was proposing would be a good way to start things. He said he would get the party organized and would then notify all the Irish relatives. He said all of them would be able to drive to Clonmel on a weekend, and he was confident that they would be anxious to do so. He said we could split the cost, but I told him that this party was on me and not to concern himself with that aspect. He reluctantly agreed.

About two weeks later, Fergus called to inform us that P. J. had died suddenly in his sleep and that a big funeral was scheduled because he had been a civic leader for so many years. Fergus had heard nothing about any party for Joseph and Liliana, so I assumed that nothing had been done—that turned out to be the case.

All of us were disappointed. Joseph had met Áine and Fiona, two of P. J.'s daughters, and their husbands when they visited the States several years before. But meeting only those four was just a tip of the iceberg. There were another twenty or so that I wanted him to get to know. With P. J.'s family grieving as you might expect, this was no time to plan a big party. Those introductions would have to wait … maybe next year.

I was shocked by P. J.'s death. Even though he was overweight and crippled by his bad hip, he was apparently in good health. He was always looking ahead. He was still a stern father to his seven children, but he was a pushover for his grandchildren. He loved his family, and it was obvious to Mary and me that his affection for kinfolk extended to us. He had gone out of his way to welcome us into the extended Jones family, and was excited when he arranged for the Mayor's Reception on our second trip to Ireland in 1989. Between our trips to Ireland when we talked over the long distance telephone lines, he would ask: *John, when are you coming home?* In his eyes, Ireland was our home—we were temporarily residing in America.

He had many, many friends in Clonmel, County Tipperary, and across Ireland. His political adversaries in *Fianna Fail* disagreed but respected his viewpoints, and they wished he was the stalwart in their party that he was in *Fine Gael.*

Even though he is gone, I can picture him now: wearing his ever-present fisherman's sweater, sitting on the front edge of his chair with both hands resting atop his upright aluminum cane, his gold-rimmed glasses resting loosely on his nose, his conversation always enjoyable. He could be a showman expressing himself, but he was a good listener as well. It was always fun being with P. J. All who knew him, miss him—things just aren't the same in Old Bridge.

His friends turned out in the hundreds for his funeral service. P. J.'s death shocked the city fathers as much as it did his family, and it took several days to arrange an appropriate service for a longtime civic leader. He is buried in St. Patrick's Cemetery in Clonmel.

*   *   *   *

WHILE WRITING THIS final chapter, I tried to analyze all the events we have recorded and to consider the contributions that members of the extended family have made. A family is only as close as its members will allow it to be. We have felt so lucky that we were able to trace those relatives whom we have chronicled in this book.

In looking back, Joanna Jones King—the Mother of the Year—stands very tall. She was the one who brought my great-grandparents out of their bad situation and financed their emigration from Tipperary. She was the one who stepped up to the plate when the eight children of her late sister were dumped into an orphanage. She was the one who shouldered the burden of being mother to thirteen, nursing them from very early ages to maturity. She was the one who maintained extremely close ties to her King family children as they chose to remain in the

Hannibal area. She was the one whom my grandmother, Nellie, my dad, and my uncles, Mike and Bob, always referred to as "Aunt Jo." Her death in 1936 left a big hole in our family, but the love and devotion she had shown to so many quickly filled that hole—and we are left with memories that will last with each of us as long as we are still here.

*   *   *   *

THE CENSUS BUREAU has reported that forty-five million Americans claim Irish heritage. Some of those have relatives who emigrated from Northern Ireland, and they mostly claim Scotch-Irish blood. It was Presbyterians from Scotland who were given land grants to move across the narrow straits to Ireland many years ago, and they were the forefathers of the American Scotch-Irish.

But a majority of those claiming Irish ancestors are descendents of those who were forced to leave because of the potato famine, the lack of opportunity, religious persecution, or the attitude of the Protestant English landlords toward the Catholic Irish underclass—an attitude that lasted eight hundred years. Before deciding to emigrate, they had been denied the right to vote and the right to own property. They were truly the underclass, but their self-esteem and their ethic of hard work came back to life when they arrived in America or Australia.

Stories about individuals or families emigrating either to America or Australia are embedded in the Irish. Virtually all families living in the twenty-six counties of Ireland and the six counties in Northern Ireland have relatives in the States, but unfortunately, most of those American relatives know very little about their ancestors still living across the Atlantic. I'm certain that many would love to know about their Irish family—they probably have wondered how they got to where they are.

That was how Mary and I felt when we started our genealogical research nearly twenty years ago. We wanted to find out who my relatives were and where they lived. We wanted to meet them, and we wanted to know them. We hoped that we would ultimately be accepted back into the same family that our ancestors had left when they immigrated to America.

We feel that we have accomplished all of that.

And we encourage other Americans like ourselves to search out their Irish roots. They can hire genealogical research companies to do the work for them, or they can do what we did: get a few basic facts together and go from there. The heritage centers in most of the twenty-six counties are available to help. You can get passenger lists from the coffin ships that brought many immigrants to the States, and you can get information from Ellis Island files. Much information is only a Google away on your home computer. The Church of Jesus Christ of Latter-day Saints, also known as the Mormon Church, maintains extensive files, which are also available on the Internet.

Our family was separated nearly 125 years ago because of emigration, but now our family stretches from Tipperary to Texas. We may be miles apart but we have reunited into one family once again. It is a wonderful feeling.

We discovered that Ireland is truly in my blood. And it is in the blood of my children.

Thanks again, Aunt Jo.

Acknowledgments

WRITING AND PREPARING a book for a publisher is not a one-man job. As the author of *Tipperary to Texas,* there is no way that I could have completed the task without a huge amount of help from other people—friends and relatives alike.

From reading this book, you know by now just how important my wife, Mary, has been. She has encouraged—even nagged—me to record our research in this book, and she has helped immeasurably by recording events, building the family tree, scrambling through old family letters and folders, and keeping in touch with our Irish kinfolk.

Our son, Jem Welsh, who resides with his family in San Clemente, California, has been a sounding board for the compilation of the various chapters. He assisted in researching and compiling portions of the Ireland and Texas Connection section. He is an author himself, writing primarily about nutrition. He has been very supportive of me.

My college roommate and friend for over sixty years, Frank Mangan, and his wife, Judy, have been very helpful leading up to and anxious for this book's publication. They are retired book publishers (and authors, themselves), and know their former trade very well. Their copyreading and editing, their suggestions, their comments, and their compliments, along with their overall sincere support, have been very encouraging to me. Without them, there would be no book. They are real professionals.

John Bauer, another longtime friend and a former business associate, is a print shop pro. He knows printing, photography, and graphic arts, and when the final submission of this manuscript was ready to go, John was the computer genius who formatted the chapters and the front and back pages into a manuscript, and then did the uploading to my publisher. It was not easy for him to deal with a PC dodo like me, but he did it. Thanks, John.

Gathering and verifying some of the information within this book had to be done via the Internet and long distance telephone. Michael O'Connor of the Waterford Heritage Services helped speed along two research commissions I gave him. He used both the computerized files at his research center and records at the Civil Registry in Waterford. He was quick to remind me that it is easier and quicker to trace the older records than it is the new ones, which have not been computerized yet.

Kathleen Crowley, a lovely lady to talk with and a valuable volunteer from the Adare Heritage Center, provided me with a wealth of information about Holy Trinity Abbey in Adare village in County Limerick, Ireland.

When I first contacted iUniverse, Inc. about publishing this book, I was directed to Molly O'Bryan, who was a breath of fresh air. If I had questions and couldn't readily find my assigned contact person, Molly was right there to help. My appreciation goes out to Molly and my manuscript editor and cover graphics artist for their dedication to my project.

A good book is the result of adequate writing and excellent editing. Susanne Lif, a publishing services associate at iUniverse, Inc., has kept this project running smoothly.

My final editor, Maera Winters, probably grew weary from making suggestions and recommending changes—she knows her business, and any author publishing through iUniverse, Inc., will be fortunate to have her expertise available to him.

Kudos go to Joyce Greenfield and the design services crew of iUniverse who turned my manuscript into a book.

Last, but not least, my thanks to my cousin, Fiona O'Keeffe, in Naas, County Kildare, Ireland. She plugged a couple of holes in my records, saving me a lot of time in final preparations to submit my manuscript.

Thanks to you all. We'll share several pints of Guinness when I next see you.

Want to Search for Your Roots?

IT IS THE author's wish that you dedicate yourself to tracing your family's history, especially if you have Irish roots. I can assure you that it will be worth the time and effort you put into it.

There are several ways of beginning the search, but it is imperative that you have at least a factual starting point, such as a relative's birth date and birthplace in Ireland. If you have that, each additional piece of information you already have—or may discover—will help you as you go through the subsequent steps in completing your search.

The easiest way, if you have that first piece of information, is to commission a reputable Irish genealogical search company. They will typically charge you an hourly fee for the time they spend on your project. This can be expensive, so be certain you discuss the amount of time the researchers expect to take. They might undertake your project for a flat fee if you have a fair amount of facts to start them with. You can find lists of Irish research firms by surfing the Internet (I suggest you enter "Ireland Genealogical Research" in a Google search). Some

Irish-American magazines and newspapers have advertisements for research firms.

Probably the most common method of searching for ancestral roots is through one of the Irish Heritage Centers located in most of the twenty-six counties of Ireland and the six counties of Northern Ireland. If you have computer access, there is one Web site that I would recommend you read and analyze—it will make your project much, much easier: www.kinsella. org/genealogy/research/irhercen.htm.

This site is kept up by the Irish Heritage Centers. Briefly, it tells you that, effective in the beginning of 2007, the charges for research by the Irish Heritage Centers has been standardized. Each center can undertake two types of commissions:

- *Full family history* research leading to a detailed report on a particular family, or

- Searches of *specified records* for specified items of information.

The Web site explains what you must do to set up their full family history search. An application fee of €10 to €15 (about $14 to $21 U.S.), together with a completed application form, is required. Then an assessment of what can be expected from the search will be made and an estimate will be provided for the amount of time likely to be required to complete the search. A quotation of costs will be made to you. These costs vary greatly from one search to another. You can expect the lower end of charges to be from €150 and up (about $215 U.S.). For the amount of the final cost, you can expect to receive a chart detailing—generation by generation—the family's descent from the earliest ancestor located to the beginning of the present century.

The Web site says this search will also provide you with facsimile documents, maps, gravestone inscriptions and other corroborative evidence. Of course, the heritage center you contact will need some factual data for a starting point.

For record searches, your heritage center can research civil records between 1864 and 1921 and church records from the parish's starting point of keeping information to present. Your costs will vary depending upon whether those records have been computerized and upon the number of households needing to be searched. Searches can also include old census records for one surname within a given parish or within the entire county.

In every search, a printout of all information found is furnished to you.

You can submit your application and arrange your search by telephone from the U.S. to the appropriate Irish Heritage Center. All of the heritage centers are listed on the Web site, complete with mailing address, telephone number, e-mail address, and the name of the person in charge of each center. You can pay for your charges with a credit card.

Inside Ireland (www.insideireland.com) is a quarterly printed publication that is knowledgeable and informative about many matters concerning Ireland. We depended upon facts it provided when Mary and I were planning our relocation in 1996. Several years ago, it started a bi-monthly e-mail newsletter for a very reasonable subscription price, and the September 2007 issue provides additional sources if you are searching you roots.

It reports "The civil or State registration of marriages, other than Catholic marriages, commenced in Ireland in 1845. In 1864, civil registration of all births, marriages, and deaths began. These civil records are held at the General Register Office, Joyce House, Lombard Street, Dublin 2. Telephone

+353-635-4000. E-mail www.gro.ie. First, dial 011 for international long distance from the U. S.

"Microfilm copies (of church records) usually up to the year 1880 of most surviving Catholic parish registers are available for consultation in the National Library of Ireland. For the start-dates of relevant registers and microfilm numbers, consult the *List of Parish registers*. (Copies of the list may be consulted in the Catalogue Room in the Geneology Service, and on the Library's Web site at www.nli.ie. Most registers may be freely consulted. However, in the case of two dioceses—Cashel and Emly and Kerry—letters of authorization must be obtained prior to consultation of the microfilms.)" [Author's note: you could substitute the word *consult* with *review* or *refer*.]

Or you can use a combination of methods like we did. Fortunately, we had many facts to use as starting points, and those served as a broad outline for our search. We supplemented those facts with data obtained from a heritage center. In one case, we visited the heritage center in person during a trip to Ireland, and in another instance, we obtained information by discussing the information we needed by long distance telephone and e-mailing the heritage center.

One other avenue: you can find several outstanding books dealing specifically with roots research. Look these up at Amazon.com or on the Barnes & Noble Web site, or check with the information desk at any major bookseller.

Don't let this research overwhelm you. Once you start, it will be easy. Yes, it can cost a reasonable sum of money, but you will have the opportunity to budget it as you go along, particularly with a heritage center, since its staff will give you their estimated (maybe even exact) costs when you discuss your needs with them.

Get going. What you find will be rewarding to you. More importantly, it will be invaluable to your descendents.

The Ireland and Texas
Connection

WHILE DOING MY research for this book, I was pleasantly surprised to find many interesting facts connecting Ireland to Texas. Although these links have no direct relationship to the four families featured in this book, I thought it would be a valued addition for the benefit of readers, since each should have a personal interest in either Ireland or Texas, or both. Like one of my high school teachers said, "History is not just something old that happened, it is something old that happened that you need to remember." Good point.

The Irish Settle in Texas

PRIMARILY CAUSED BY the brutal English subjugation, the massive emigration in the eighteenth and nineteenth centuries led many Irish families to Texas. Natives of Ireland were among the first settlers in Spanish-ruled Texas, and they played important roles in the development of the state.

Probably the first Irishman in Texas was Hugh O'Connor, who fled from Dublin to Mexico via Spain. He succeeded in reinforcing San Antonio against marauding Apaches, and in appreciation for his leadership, Spanish authorities changed his surname to Oconór and appointed him governor ad interim of Texas in 1767. He went on to become an important leader for Spain in the New World, serving in other high posts in Mexico and in Cuba.

Philip Nolan, a native of Belfast, was the first Anglo American to map Texas. In 1801, his mapping and surveying activities aroused suspicion among Spanish authorities, and he was killed by a force that had been sent to arrest him.

Of the ninety-one Texans who signed the Goliad Declaration of Independence from Mexico in 1835, twenty-five were Irishmen. Four natives of Ireland put their signatures on the official Texas Declaration of Independence that was signed in 1836 at the town of Washington-on-the-Brazos. This important document set off the battle for Texas independence, and large Mexican armies, led by President Santa Anna, marched across the Rio Grande to put down the rebellion.

Fierce battles raged at both the Alamo in San Antonio and Goliad, but the final encounter at San Jacinto ended in a victory for the Texans and their leader, Sam Houston. He listed one hundred Irishmen on the roster of his seven hundred-man force.

The 1850 census, including Texas for the first time after it became a State, showed 1403 Irish in Texas. By 1860, the census number had grown to 3480, and the Irish continued to settle in Texas. The 2000 census, the most recent, shows 1,502,841 Irish—almost 8 percent of the overall total of 20,851,820 Texans.

The Colonies at Refugio and San Patricio

ABOUT 1828, THE Mexican government issued *empresario* contracts that granted four Irishmen the right to colonize an area in Texas now known as Refugio and San Patricio counties. James Hewetson, a physician, and his associate, James Power, recruited several hundred families from County Wexford in Ireland to move to their colony at Refugio.

Coincidentally, John McMullen and James McGloin were also given approval to solicit new settlers for their colony at nearby San Patricio at the same time. Another contract was issued to a Mexican named DeLeón for a colony at Victoria. According to the University of Texas' *Handbook of Texas Online,* the contacts stated that the Refugio and the Victoria colonies be settled by Mexican and Irish families, specifically Catholics. This was not included in the San Patricio contract.

Irish at the Alamo

IF YOU SAW John Wayne courting the redheaded Maureen O'Hara in *The Quiet Man*, and then saw Wayne portray the famed Davy Crockett in *The Alamo* epic, it is easy to relate the Irish to the Alamo. The truth is, however, there was more than just the *Duke*. Since there were no survivors to let us know details about the victims, we must rely on historians and researchers. *The Handbook of Texas Online,* compiled by the University of Texas at Austin, says that eleven native Irishmen were killed at the Alamo.

Many of the officers at the Alamo were second- and third-generation Irish. They were not alone. In 1836, there were more than one thousand first-generation Irish immigrants living in Texas.

"Los San Patricios"

RESEARCH ABOUT THE Irish who became a part of the St. Patrick's Battalion *(Los San Patricios)* raises this question: Do you regard a group of Irish who had settled in a part of Mexico called Texas as heroes or traitors after they fought for the Mexicans in the U.S.-Mexico War of 1846-1848?

Historians are split. *The Handbook of Texas Online*, developed by the University of Texas at Austin and the Texas State Historical Association, and a San Carlos, Mexico, Web site present somewhat different views of the war. However, both seem plausible—you decide. Briefly, here's the story:

There are many reasons the U.S. invaded Mexico in 1846 (after Texas had been admitted as a State), but the main reason was probably that the U.S. wanted the huge chunk of Mexican territory that is now the desert Southwest (roughly New Mexico, Arizona, Nevada, and California, plus parts of Colorado and Utah) primarily for its minerals, the Pacific Coast ports, and the trade routes through what is now New Mexico. The U.S. offered millions of dollars to purchase the territory, but Mexico refused to sell it. General Ulysses Grant believed that the invasion was not justified, but General Winfield Scott sent his troops streaming into Mexico from Texas and from an amphibious landing at Veracruz.

There were many Irishmen fighting for the U.S. Historians say that one of four men in the Army was Irish. There were seventeen wholly Irish companies that saw action, including such decorated units as the Emmet Guards from New York, the Jasper Greens from Georgia, the Mobile Volunteers from Alabama, and the Hibernian Greens from Pennsylvania. But, as happened during the Civil War, the Irish fought on both sides.

There were defectors. Some Irish enlistees began to feel that they were fighting on the side of injustice. They saw the U.S. carrying out a greedy and cruel land grab—reminding them of the English occupation of Ireland. Others supported Mexico because the Mexicans were Catholic. Many of the Irish recalled the immigrant bashing when they arrived in the U.S. from Ireland, and they did not want to be on the side of exploiters, expansionists, religious bigots, or slave owners. Still others were attracted by higher pay.

The St. Patrick's Battalion was formed early on in the war, led by John Riley who had deserted from the U.S. Army before the war began. Members of the battalion fought heroically and aggressively, participating in all the major battles of the war. They were cited for bravery by General Santa Anna, commander and president of Mexico. In one of the last battles of the war, the Irishmen fought until their ammunition was exhausted. They tore down the white flag of surrender that was raised by their Mexican comrades, preferring to fight on with bayonets.

When the war ended, eighty-five Irishmen were captured and, historians report, seventy-two received a court martial. General Scott eventually issued some pardons, but thirty were hanged as traitors. Because of a technicality, the leader Riley was not hanged, but received 50 lashes and the letter "D" for deserter was branded on his cheek.

This did not end the story of *Los San Patricios*. Mexico continued to recruit deserters, and formed two more companies. After the war, they continued as a group, patrolling Mexico to protect the people from bandits and Indians. When they were disbanded at the end of 1848, many asked the Mexican government for assistance in moving back to their European homelands, but most remained in Mexico because they could not return to the United States.

Mexico continues to honor *Los San Patricios* as national heroes, referring to them as "Irish martyrs." Today, many Mexicans still have not forgotten the outcome and horror of the war, and many claim sovereignty over the huge parcel of land that the U.S. seized, but ultimately bought.

On the other hand, many American historians regard the troops of the St. Patrick's Battalion as traitors who deserted their units and fully deserved the treatment they received at the war's end.

Shamrock, Texas

IN 1890, AN Irish immigrant sheepherder named George Nickel applied to open a post office at his dugout home six miles north of the present town site and suggested the name Shamrock for good luck and courage. The post office never opened because Nickel's home burned out, but the name for the town stuck and another post office was established nearby. However, the town of Shamrock, Texas, did not get its official beginning until the Chicago/Rock Island/Gulf railway arrived in the summer of 1892.

Dreaded Tuberculosis

MANY MEMBERS OF the Jones/Powell/Welsh/King families have died of tuberculosis since the 1850s. Tuberculosis was one of the most feared and dreaded diseases of that era, and there was no medicinal remedy. Many children perished from the disease in the first few years after their birth. Physicians recommended bed rest and hospitalization in high altitude, low humidity areas—advice that is hardly applicable to Ireland.

Many immigrants to America were moved to Texas, primarily West Texas. Between 1892 and 1925, twelve private sanatoriums opened—in El Paso alone—and another fifty beds were set aside for "lungers" at Hotel Dieu, a private Catholic hospital in El Paso.

The "Undesirables"

THE UNITED STATES got its nickname "The Melting Pot" because ethnic groups flocked to the States during the nineteenth, twentieth, and twenty-first centuries. These closely-knit groups have all suffered through the same bigotry before finally being accepted for what they have become: Americans. Until recent years, most of these groups have been from Europe—but few, if any, were more discriminated against than the Irish.

The Irish came in large families, they had few resources, and they had few skills. They could communicate, but their brogue was hard to understand, even though they spoke English. There was one other thing the Irish all shared—they were used to hard work. But as they searched for jobs, they continually encountered prejudice. "No Irish Need Apply" signs were everywhere they went.

Some 15 percent of the population in 1910 was foreign born, and that number was rising. People of all races were coming from not only Ireland, but also from Italy, Poland, Germany, Russia, and Sweden, to name some. Jews came from many nations. The Asians that came were mainly Chinese. Immigrants were simply a despised class of people.

Years before he became president, the scholarly Woodrow Wilson described immigrants as being of the "lowest class" and coming from "sordid and hapless elements." Those comments can be found in a book he wrote in 1902, and by today's standards, they were not politically correct.

Except for African Americans, the prejudice against the Irish lasted longer than against other ethnic groups, probably because there were so many Irish coming in. Many settled in New York City and Boston ghetto neighborhoods, living in crowded, unsanitary tenements. Some families lived in one room; others were jammed into apartments with relatives or friends from back home. But other Irish immigrants moved west, seeking work in places like Chicago, Minneapolis, Philadelphia, St. Louis, Memphis, and Pittsburgh. Still others followed their relatives to the coal mines in Appalachia or to farms in the Midwest or the South.

It is easy to understand why so many politicians of Irish descent are out in front for the reform of American immigration laws—their ancestors and those of their constituents went through many of the same problems that today's immigrants face.

The Harp and Shamrock Society

WITH SO MANY Irish living along the East Coast, it is no surprise that the St. Patrick's Day parade in New York City gets most of the attention of the media and oftentimes excites controversy. But there are seventy-plus parades on March 17 each year honoring St. Patrick, and they take place across the U.S., stretching from New York to Atlanta to Los Angeles and on to Seattle. Of course, there is the mother (or would it be father?) of all St. Patrick's Day parades in Dublin, and there are also marching celebrations in Tokyo and London.

But the Harp and Shamrock Society of San Antonio has made sure that Texas is not left out in honoring Ireland's patron priest. This dedicated group of Ireland lovers has been honoring St. Patrick for almost forty years now.

Two professors and a graduate student of St. Mary's University in San Antonio met in 1966 to discuss a mutual concern. Irish-born Dr. Seán Burke got together with third-generation Irish emigrant, retired Air Force colonel, and graduate student, Joseph McShane; and first-generation Irish emigrant, scientist, and instructor at the U.S. Air Force School of Aerospace Medicine, Patrick Dowd, to form a group that would "involve persons of Irish nationality or heritage to do honor to the land of their forefathers."

They established a long set of goals to recognize Irishmen who have made contributions to Texas beginning with the first colonization of early Texas to the present. They aim to attain a fuller appreciation of the cultural achievements of Ireland. They strive to preserve Irish architecture from the 1830s; establish historic landmarks and cultural centers; assist local museums and libraries to offer past and present Irish literature; recognize contributions of the Irish in music, art, literature, and theater; publish a journal with appropriate articles that further the society's goals; hold monthly meetings and regular social events for members; and host Irish dignitaries—as well as organize a St. Patrick's Day Parade and the ceremonies to be held at the Alamo in downtown San Antonio. The society is nonsectarian, charitable, cultural, civic, educational, patriotic, and social.

The society's first St. Patrick's Day parade took place in 1968 with 250 marchers who plodded about four blocks to the Alamo. From that humble beginning, the parade has grown in interest and participation, and more than twenty thousand marchers and nearly one hundred thousand viewers have taken part.

Beginning in 1969—the second year—the group joined together with the Paseo Del Rio Association to dye the San Antonio River a Kelly green color and rename it "The River Shannon" for one day. Since then, the group has continued the festival with a special Irish show of song, dance, and music. One of their festivals and fund-raising efforts benefits a long list of San Antonio area organizations and scholarships, and honors one person by naming him or her The Irishman of the Year. The society presents the honoree with the Cuchulainn statue of bronze mounted on Connemara marble. A building fund has been established to raise funds for the society's cultural and social center to serve the San Antonio area. Its Web site is kept current and is very informative—visit *www.harpandsham-rock.org.*

Bibliography

IN PUTTING TOGETHER the short *Time Capsules* placed between chapters of this book, and *The Ireland and Texas Connection* which combines several footnotes to history, I obtained some tidbits and verified some of the information from various books and online websites. I appreciate these sources, and recommend them to readers:

A Short Guide to Your Genealogical Search.
http://www.insideireland.com/genealogy.htm September 2007

Bruun, Erik and Jay Crosby, eds. *Living History of America: The History of the United States in Documents, Essays, Letters, Songs and Poems.* New York: Tess Press, 1999.

Kathy Weiser, Owner/Editor "Shamrock-Texas Main Street" *Texas Legends*
http://legendsofamerica.com/TX-Shamrock.html (Accessed October 24, 2007)

Kee, Robert. *Ireland, A History.* Great Britain: Abacus, 2003

Our History. *The Harp and Shamrock Society.*
http://harpandshamrock.org/history.html (Accessed October 24, 2007)

Texas State Historical Association. "Health and Medicine." *The Handbook of Texas Online.*
http://tsha.utexas.edu/handbook/online/articles/HH/smhzu.html (Accessed July 21, 2007)

Texas State Historical Association. "Irish." *The Handbook of Texas Online.* http://www.tsha.utexas.edu/handbook/online/articles/II/piil.html. (Accessed July 21, 2007)

Texas State Historical Association. "San Patricio Battalion." *The Handbook of Texas Online.*
http://www.tsha.utexas.edu/handbook/online/articles/SS/qis1_print.html (Accessed October 24, 2007)

The Mexican-American War (1846-1848).
http://www.vivasancarlos.com/ma_war.html (Accessed October 24, 2007)

*Why They Defected.*http://www.vivasancarlos.com/defected.html (Accessed October 24, 2007)

Family Trees

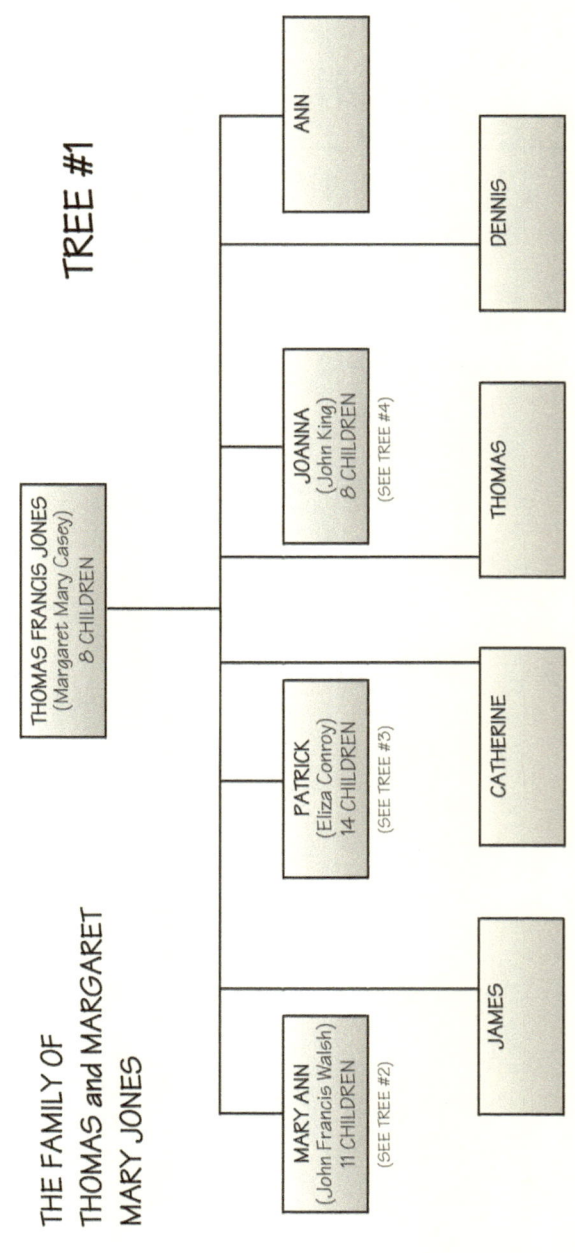

THE FAMILY OF
THOMAS and MARGARET
MARY JONES

TREE #1

THOMAS FRANCIS JONES
(Margaret Mary Casey)
8 CHILDREN

MARY ANN
(John Francis Walsh)
11 CHILDREN
(SEE TREE #2)

PATRICK
(Eliza Conroy)
14 CHILDREN
(SEE TREE #3)

JOANNA
(John King)
8 CHILDREN
(SEE TREE #4)

ANN

JAMES

CATHERINE

THOMAS

DENNIS

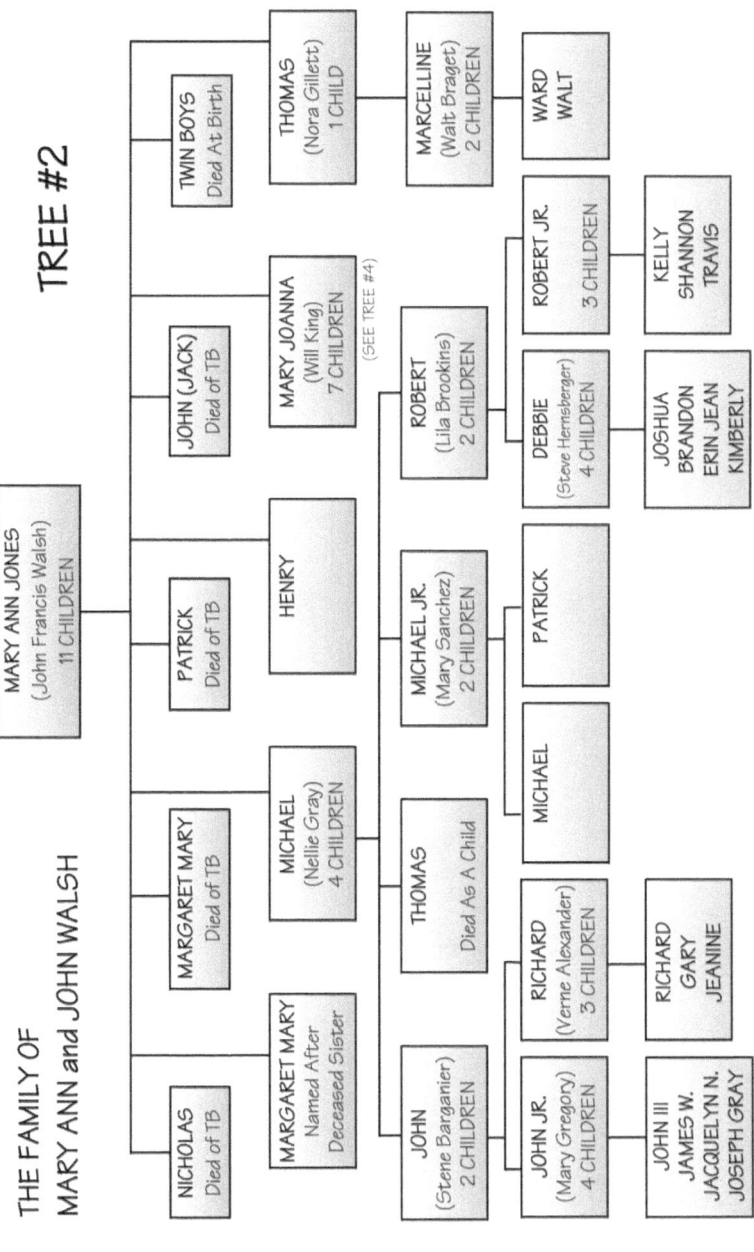

TREE #2

THE FAMILY OF
MARY ANN and JOHN WALSH

MARY ANN JONES
(John Francis Walsh)
11 CHILDREN

NICHOLAS
Died of TB

MARGARET MARY
Named After Deceased Sister

MARGARET MARY
Died of TB

PATRICK
Died of TB

JOHN (JACK)
Died of TB

TWIN BOYS
Died At Birth

MICHAEL
(Nellie Gray)
4 CHILDREN

HENRY

MARY JOANNA
(Will King)
7 CHILDREN
(SEE TREE #4)

THOMAS
(Nora Gillett)
1 CHILD

JOHN
(Steve Barganier)
2 CHILDREN

THOMAS
Died As A Child

MICHAEL JR.
(Mary Sanchez)
2 CHILDREN

ROBERT
(Lila Brookins)
2 CHILDREN

MARCELLINE
(Walt Braget)
2 CHILDREN

JOHN JR.
(Mary Gregory)
4 CHILDREN

RICHARD
(Verne Alexander)
3 CHILDREN

MICHAEL

PATRICK

DEBBIE
(Steve Hemsberger)
4 CHILDREN

ROBERT JR.
3 CHILDREN

WARD
WALT

JOHN III
JAMES W.
JACQUELYN N.
JOSEPH GRAY

RICHARD
GARY
JEANINE

JOSHUA
BRANDON
ERIN JEAN
KIMBERLY

KELLY
SHANNON
TRAVIS

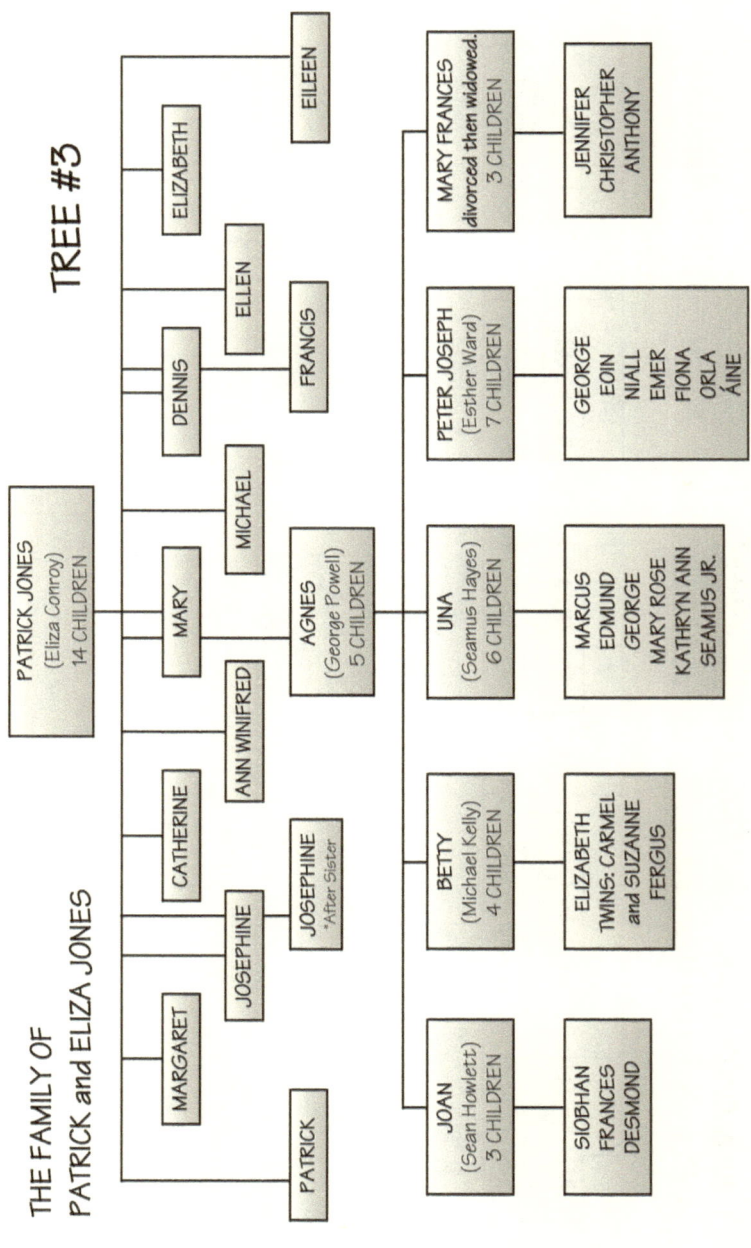

TREE #3

THE FAMILY OF PATRICK and ELIZA JONES

PATRICK JONES
(Eliza Conroy)
14 CHILDREN

PATRICK — MARGARET — JOSEPHINE — CATHERINE — ANN WINIFRED — MARY — DENNIS — ELIZABETH — EILEEN

JOSEPHINE — JOSEPHINE *After Sister* — MICHAEL — ELLEN

AGNES
(George Powell)
5 CHILDREN — FRANCIS

JOAN
(Sean Howlett)
3 CHILDREN

SIOBHAN
FRANCES
DESMOND

BETTY
(Michael Kelly)
4 CHILDREN

ELIZABETH
TWINS: CARMEL
and SUZANNE
FERGUS

UNA
(Seamus Hayes)
6 CHILDREN

MARCUS
EDMUND
GEORGE
MARY ROSE
KATHRYN ANN
SEAMUS JR.

PETER JOSEPH
(Esther Ward)
7 CHILDREN

GEORGE
EOIN
NIALL
EMER
FIONA
ORLA
ÁINE

MARY FRANCES
divorced then widowed.
3 CHILDREN

JENNIFER
CHRISTOPHER
ANTHONY

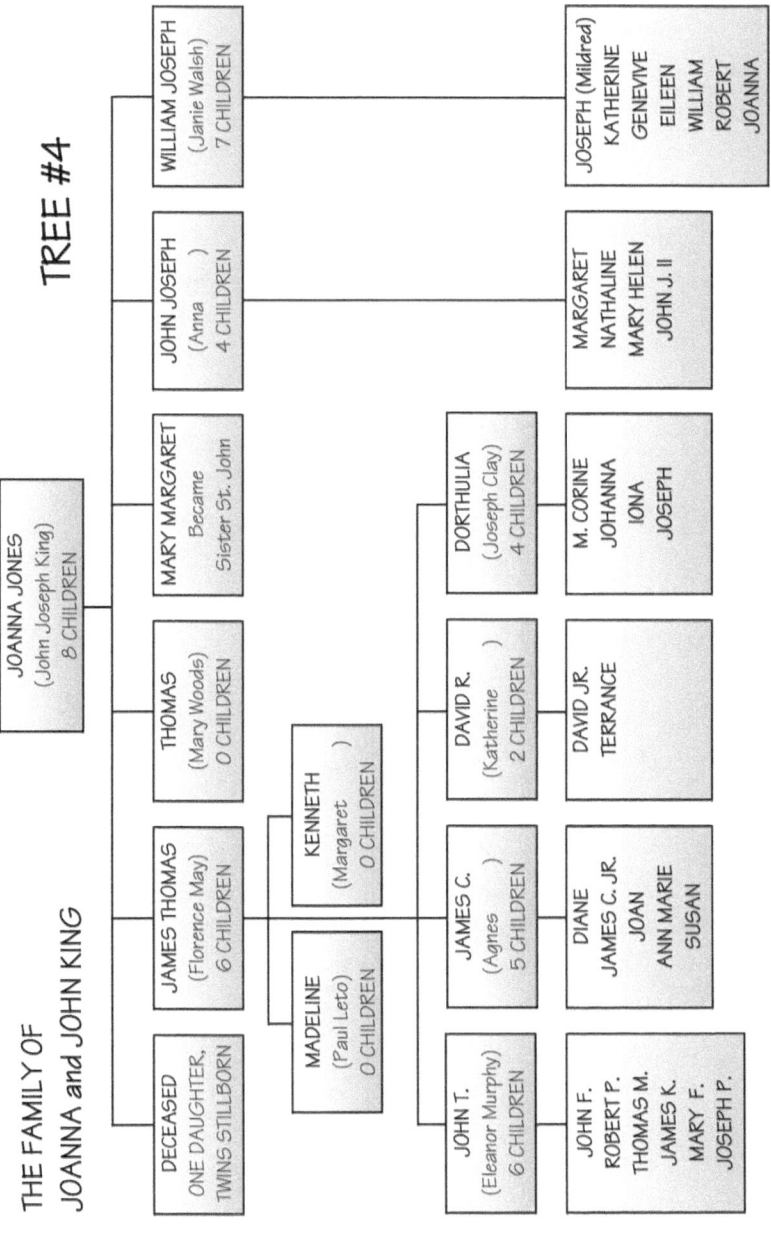

TREE #4

THE FAMILY OF JOANNA and JOHN KING

JOANNA JONES
(John Joseph King)
8 CHILDREN

DECEASED
ONE DAUGHTER,
TWINS STILLBORN

JAMES THOMAS
(Florence May)
6 CHILDREN

THOMAS
(Mary Woods)
0 CHILDREN

MARY MARGARET
Became
Sister St. John

JOHN JOSEPH
(Anna)
4 CHILDREN

WILLIAM JOSEPH
(Janie Walsh)
7 CHILDREN

MADELINE
(Paul Leto)
0 CHILDREN

KENNETH
(Margaret)
0 CHILDREN

JOHN T.
(Eleanor Murphy)
6 CHILDREN

JAMES C.
(Agnes)
5 CHILDREN

DAVID R.
(Katherine)
2 CHILDREN

DORTHULIA
(Joseph Clay)
4 CHILDREN

MARGARET
NATHALINE
MARY HELEN
JOHN J. II

JOSEPH (Mildred)
KATHERINE
GENEVIVE
EILEEN
WILLIAM
ROBERT
JOANNA

JOHN F.
ROBERT P.
THOMAS M.
JAMES K.
MARY F.
JOSEPH P.

DIANE
JAMES C. JR.
JOAN
ANN MARIE
SUSAN

DAVID JR.
TERRANCE

M. CORINE
JOHANNA
IONA
JOSEPH

978-0-595-45356-6
0-595-45356-2